SEX, DRUGS, AND VIOLENCE IN THE COMICS

D1289165

PURE IMAGINATION
N.Y.C.

SEX, DRUGS, AND VIOLENCE IN THE COMICS is tm and © 2008 by Pure Imagination Publishing, 29 Herkimer Street #2, Brooklyn, NY, 11216. 347-240-4327. All material is believed to be in the public domain, and each piece of art has been altered slightly to fingerprint this version. Unauthorized use constitutes theft of services and copyright infringement.

"Brother, can you spare a friend?"

by Greg Theakston

In 1953-54 when the Comics industry was coming under fire from censorship groups across the continent, they found that they had few friends. Not that they had many to begin with. Comic books are the direct descendants of the Pulps of the '30s, and continued the tradition of sex and violence in various doses for over a decade.

And there is another reason comics didn't have any friends: money.

In 1953, Comics were a far bigger industry than most people realized. Because Comics' content wasn't supposed to be taken seriously, the form never was either. The truth is, the Comics industry had shown steady grown every year since its inception in 1933. Twenty years later, one of every three periodicals sold in the United States was a comic book (**NEWSDEALER**, various issues 1953). Dozens of titles sold from 500,000 to 1,000,000+ copies MONTHLY, and publisher were getting rich off of businesses with a tiny overheads. On a more practical level, paper mills buzzed with activity, ink manufacturers were at capacity, printing plants and the thousands who worked there were guaranteed a steady check, delivery-men got a piece of the action, and the mom-and-pop stores enjoyed the steady jingle of coins into the register. It was a money-chain of dimes.

Then the cash cow dried up overnight.

And everybody felt it.

A multi-billion dollar business shriveled-up in the blink of an eye, and it didn't make a blip on the radar. The media never addressed the economic disaster the hearings had wrought, and with good reason. The other media wanted the comics dead. Every dime spent by an adult on a comic was a dime not spent on **READER'S DIGEST**. Every dime spent by a kid for a comic was a dime that wouldn't buy a movie. Television wanted kids' attention to enjoy Three Stooges reruns and beg mom to buy whatever the commercials hawked. Newspapers wanted their comic strip children readers back.

It's easy to see why Comics didn't have any friends in 1954: Money.

And so after the Congressional hearings in April of 1954, a multi-billion dollar business was instantly dead on the vine. Fruits of twenty years of publishing decimated in a little more than a season, and virtually nothing was ever reported about it. Comics never had a very good reputation, and after the hearings, it was seemingly tarnished forever. Television and movies decided that comics would make for good comedy relief, and when a character was portrayed as simple-minded they inevitably mentioned their comic book collection.

Weird Mysteries #5 (June 1953) features a cover that crosses the borders of good taste.

Above: "A French-kiss from the grave" from **CHAMBER OF CHILLS #23 (May 1954)**.
Right: "Cold Turkey" from **SHOCK SUSPENSE STORIES #12 (Dec. 1953)**.

The rest of the media simply ignored the form all together, until the late-1960s, then only to amaze the public with the fact that **ACTION COMICS #1** was worth $100. Comics never did recover from the Congressional Hearings of 1954, not even fifty years later.

So what was all the fuss about?

In an effort to win readers' dimes, the comics of the late '40s and early '50s, published by the smaller companies, pushed the envelope. While 21st century eyes may not be that startled at the doings, we must put things in perspective: At the time, you didn't see much blood at the movies, and certainly not on television. This vile stuff was being issued to a sanitized public, children especially.

However, like on the **TWILIGHT ZONE**, these are cautionary tales. Not as it is destined to be but as it might be if you changed your terrible direction, if the person in the story is you.

"Don't do bad things to people, lest bad things happen to you."

E.C. Publisher William Gaines should have made that argument at the hearings.

"What? Are you just looking at the pictures, or you actually reading this thing. We publish sensational art, but there is a lesson in every story."

Like the O'Henry tradition.

"Terrible things happen to terrible people."

It was preachy era. Lots of talk about Sin. Lots of judgement, and an attempt to explain why the kids were running wild. And, if you want to see what was worrying shrinks and parents alike, read on.
GT
N.Y.C.
April, 2008

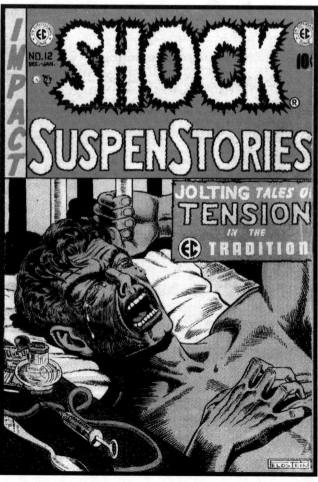

CONTENTS REVIEW

"I Was a Racket Girl for the Hollywood Stars" from **TRUE CRIME COMICS** #5 (Apr. 1947).

This volume kicks-off with a fairly early depiction of drug use in the comics. It reads like a standard B-movie from the period, like many of them do. Gloria, desperate to become a star takes on temp work as a reefer salesgirl. She gets her brother involved and he gets hooked. In the end, dreams are shattered, tears shed. All because of reefer.

Considering some of the trash that was passing for entertainment in the crime comics of the period, the story is fairly well told, and very text heavy. This was typical with both crime and romance comics of the period because publishers thought it better balanced the reading experience for the adult market. A cross between picture stories and non-fiction text executed in an attempt to draw a more literate reader. The trend lasted for a while, but ultimately comics settled on a much leaner script size.

The story is notable for containing the line "All Hell's breaking in Hollywood!" Graphic horror and suggested sexuality were the norm during the period, but language like this was unheard of. I've never seen another example in the comics, but odds are it only happened a few times, but certainly not after the Comics Code rules went into effect in 1954.

"Murder, Morphine and Me" from **TRUE CRIME** #2 (May 1947).

Speaking of graphic, Jack Cole's stories in this title are packed with violence, depravity, and characters who elicit only pity. Cole had found success with his creation Plastic Man, but he was really a well rounded artist who could depict a more straight style of story, and while not as broad as the cartoon work, this approach is still packed with flex and spring.

Told in first-person, it's Film Noir with balloons and panels. Unlike in "Racket Girl," Gloria can't wait to make a lot easy money and become famous, Mary gets sucked into the world of dope smuggling because of her lover for the sketchy Tony, and is more sympathetic because of it.

From the splash page with a guy getting impaled on a hypodermic needle through to the end of the story Cole never pulls a punch. Fresh corpses in a car, and old ones just under a vulture punctuate the shoot-outs, and work-overs. All of this is topped by a panel where the girl is being threatened in the eye with a needle, and was used in Wertham's **SEDUCTION OF THE INNOCENT** picture section.

"I Was A Come-On Girl for Broken Bones Inc." from **JUSTICE TRAPS THE GUILTY** #1 (Oct. 1947)

More sex and violence as Joe Simon and Jack Kirby get hard-boiled for a moment. Comics' top team had landed at Prize Comics right around the time crime comics were exploding, and **HEADLINE** was switched from an open format to solid crime stories. It sold so well that Prize launched a second crime title **JUSTICE TRAPS THE GUILTY** shortly after. The cover depicted a man in the electric-chair not ready for his last sizzling heart-beat. "The issue sold out because of that cover," artist Jack Kirby remembered. "Nobody'd ever seen anything like it."

"Bobby Sox Bandit Queen" from **HEADLINE COMICS** #27 (Nov. 1947)

Another Simon and Kirby effort which deals with juvenile delinquency, featuring Stella May Dickson, a fifteen-year-old who is seduced into a life of crime. She even looks like Tracy Lords.

At thirteen pages the boys really stretch out with the story, but they were also the editors so who was going to stop them?

"Satan's Cigarettes" from **WANTED COMICS** #18 (Feb. 1949)

Want another hit? Hit story?

You've got it.

This one is illustrated by Jerry Robinson, one-time top **BATMAN** artist, and inked by the very talented Mort Meskin, and is one of the better produced crime tales from this period. Not much of a story: a tobacconist is tricked into peddling dope and the bloody results that follow. But, that's what happens when you mix guns with Ganja.

"Gang Sweetheart" from **YOUNG ROMANCE** #23 (Jul. 1950)

Our third Simon and Kirby story is penciled and inked by Jack to great effect. Unlike the previous two jobs Kirby dedicates the story far more to character development rather than action situations. The result is a far more satisfying read in terms of our personal understanding of the players and their problems.

Urban drama was one of Kirby's specialties because he'd lived through it as a kid.

"Reform School Girl" from **REFORM SCHOOL GIRL** (1951)

This was the lead story in a one-shot comic of the same name. Note that the lead female isn't mentioned by until the end of page three! As usual, it's a man who leads her astray, but in this case she goes willingly.

TRAPPED! (1951)

This was an anti-drug give-away which was widely distributed to high schools of the time. While not as sordid as some of these tales, it still packs a punch. The "hero" is Bill who gets his first high in the boys' lavatory with a reefer. From there he escalates to sniffing heroin, and then shooting it. His grades and mood change, and he ends up knocking his old man down during an argument. Plenty of babes get knocked down during these stories, but his dad? Must be a junkie.

"Opium Slaves of Venus" from **CAPTAIN SCIENCE** #1 (Spr. 1951)

In an effort not to be left out, Captain Science also goes after drug dealers, though this time in space ships, with ray guns blasting death.

The art is a formative effort by Wallace Wood: not up to standard, but "B+" work for sure.

You'd think that if they could get Opium to Venus, they might be able to come up with a less addictive drug with the same kick.

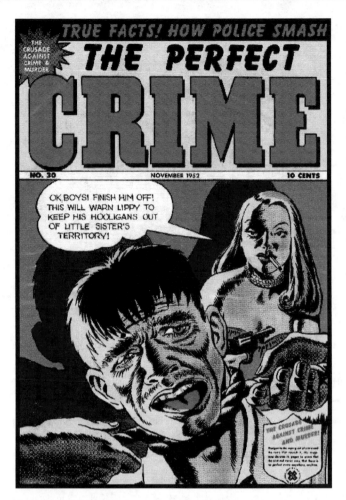

PERFECT CRIME #30 (Nov. 1952) Love stories like this choke me up too.

"Hopped Up Killer" from **FIGHT AGAINST CRIME** # 4 (Nov. 1951).

Somehow, the crude art from an unknown hand seems highly effective in the context. It's visceral in its simplicity, and begs for you to suspend your disbelief.

Look, any story that starts with "Read this true story. The evil cigarettes made him a cop-killer...but in the end..." is certainly one I want to read.

"Men in Black" from **MENACE COMICS** #3 (May 1953).

MENACE was produced by Stan Lee for Atlas' comics line, and was a response to William Gains' E.C. horror roster. Most of Atlas' other horror and mystery comics were of the cookie-cutter variety, but Lee stacked the deck with art by his top artists, and gave scripts an extra effort

John Romita, later of Spider-Man fame, does his very best art, and the work is first-class know for that you're not best-known at all.

"Three-Fold Horror and Revenge" from **FRANKENSTEIN COMICS** #32 (July 1954).

Briefer had introduced his signature character in 1940, and the monster terrorized the city for years. However, by the late-'40s the character was just a cartoon version of the original, and played strictly for laughs. In 1948, after seventeen issues in his title, the book was cancelled, but Frankenstein always comes back. In March of 1952, Prize revamped the title as a true horror series to exploit the current trend, and what followed could be pretty stark. Unlike some of the cherry-picked material in this book, almost all of the Frankenstein stories were this harsh.

"Gun Happy" from **CRIME DETECTOR** #5 (Sep 1954).

It's basically a rip-off of the movie GUN CRAZY, released early in 1951. Zero character development, little explanation to what's going on in the storyline, and art that hardly cuts it. Still, a typical example of how parents were right in thinking comics had little redeeming value.

IT'S BEST TO KNOW ABOUT ALCOHOL (1961).

This is a public service give-away comic intended to inform kids of the dangers of drinking. While reading it, you'll see that it's not very P.C., and may seem as naive as everything else in this volume. It has been abridged, because a lot of it was just boring, and I needed the space.

WHAT IF THEY CALL ME "CHICKEN?" (1970).

Another educational give-away comic. As with the other stories, the creators lay it on a little thick, though this is probably the most balanced look at drug-use in this volume. They show that the pothead is more likely to fall in front of a car than he is to kill a cop.

The art is by Jack Sparling who is best known, wait, he's not best-known for anything. Okay. **THE SECRET SIX**, but if you're best-

What follows is not the best of the exploitation comics from the '40s and '50s, because the Gaines Estate controls that, but it's a pretty clear look at the kind of comics that were causing sleepless nights from both the kids and the parents.
Greg Theakston

WE'RE OUT OF REEFERS

CONTENTS

TO PROTECT THE IDENTITY OF INNOCENT PEOPLE, SOME OF THE NAMES USED IN THIS TRUE STORY ARE FICTITIOUS

I WAS A RACKET GIRL! for the HOLLYWOOD STARS

THERE ARE A LOT OF WAYS TO WIN FAME AND FORTUNE IN HOLLYWOOD, AND MOST GIRLS WHO YEARN FOR MOVIE STARDOM GET THERE BY BEING HONEST AND SQUARE. BUT THAT WAS TOO SLOW FOR ME.! I COULDN'T WAIT FOR THE HOLLYWOOD LIGHTNING TO STRIKE ME IN THE ORDINARY WAY. I PICKED AN EASY ROUTE TO STARDOM...THE PATH OF CRIME AND DECEIT! BECAUSE I WAS GREEDY AND AMBITIOUS, I CHOSE THE TWISTED ROAD OF DOPE. I BECAME A DEALER IN MARIHUANA... DELIBERATELY... WANTONLY... SCHEMING TO MAKE USE OF THE POWER MY CONTROL OF THE TERRIBLE DRUG GAVE ME, TO FORCE MY WAY INTO THE PATH OF THE HOLLYWOOD FORTUNATES! RUTHLESSLY I SACRIFICED MY OWN CONSCIENCE, MY TRUSTING YOUNG BROTHER, MY SWEETHEART... DETERMINED THAT NOTHING WOULD STOP ME FROM REACHING THE WEALTH AND ADULATION I CRAVED. BUT BEFORE MY MAD SCHEME COULD SUCCEED, I FOUND THAT AS A WAY TO SUCCESS AND HAPPINESS, CRIME IS A FATAL MISTAKE...

"LIKE SO MANY OTHER AMBITIOUS YOUNG GIRLS, I HEADED STRAIGHT FOR HOLLYWOOD AFTER WINNING A BEAUTY CONTEST IN MY HOME TOWN. AND LIKE SO MANY OTHERS, I FOUND THE STUDIOS HARD TO CRASH. I WAS SOON REDUCED TO SLINGING HASH IN A BAR AND GRILL FOR A LIVING."

HEY, GIRLIE, HOW ABOUT A HOT CUP OF COFFEE? THIS ONE TASTES LIKE DISHWATER!

OF COURSE, SIR! RIGHT AWAY!

I'D LIKE TO POUR IT DOWN YOUR NECK, YOU JERK! HOW I HATE THIS JOB!

"THE ONLY THING THAT MADE THE JOB AT THE BLACK CAT ENDURABLE WAS JOE, THE BARTENDER. WE WERE IN LOVE WITH EACH OTHER. BUT I WAS STILL READY TO GIVE MY RIGHT EYE FOR A CHANCE IN THE MOVIES..."

SAY, GLORIA, WHO'S THAT TOUGH-LOOKING CHARACTER YOUR BOY FRIEND IS SO CHUMMY WITH?

I DON'T KNOW, MAIZIE, BUT HE'S SURE BENDING JOE'S EAR! HE LOOKS LIKE A RACKETEER OR SOMETHING! THINK I'LL WANDER OVER AND CATCH AN EARFUL FOR MYSELF!

JOE, IT'S A CINCH! WITH ALL THE MOVIE STARS THAT COME IN HERE AND SUCKERS LOOKING FOR THRILLS, YOU COULD SELL A THOUSAND DOLLARS WORTH OF REEFERS IN A WEEK! YOU MAKE THE CONTACTS WITH YOUR CUSTOMERS...I SUPPLY THE STUFF, SEE?

WELL, I DON'T KNOW-- IT'S KIND OF RISKY...

REEFERS! THAT'S MARIHUANA! AND HERE IN HOLLYWOOD THERE'S PLENTY OF DOUGH AND THE STARS GO FOR THAT THRILL STUFF!

1

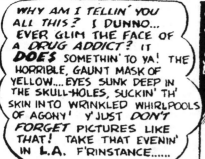

WHY AM I TELLIN' YOU ALL THIS? I DUNNO... EVER GLIM THE FACE OF A *DRUG ADDICT?* IT *DOE$* SOMETHIN' TO YA! THE HORRIBLE, GAUNT MASK OF YELLOW....EYES SUNK DEEP IN THE SKULL-HOLES, SUCKIN' TH' SKIN INTO WRINKLED WHIRLPOOLS OF AGONY! Y'JUST *DON'T FORGET* PICTURES LIKE THAT! TAKE THAT EVENIN' IN L.A. F'RINSTANCE......

MARY! YOU'VE GOT TO HELP ME! WON'T LAST THE NIGHT IF I DON'T GET MORE— *MARY!!* WAKE UP!!

G'WAY! LEMME DIE! SEE YA INNA MORNIN. Z

PLEASE, MARY! I RAN SHORT TODAY! BEEN CALLIN' YOUR NUMBER EVERY HOUR, BUT *NO ANSWER!!* TONY, THAT LIAR, SAID YOU'D LEF'T TOWN! WHY THE BRUSH? YOU *CAN'T* DROP ME NOW! YOU'VE GOTTA *TRUST* ME!

OH .. *YOU!* (YAWN) TONY MUST BE SLIPPIN', LETTIN' A SICK HOPPY JUMP HIM FOR MY ADDRESS AND LATCH-KEY! LIKE I SAID BEFORE, NO CASH, *NO DOPE!*

GIMME A BREAK! !GROAN! Y'*KNOW* I CAN'T WORK WITH THIS PAIN TEARING MY INSIDES OUT! I'LL PAY BACK EVERY CENT, ONLY I GOTTA *HAVE THE MORPHINE!!*

WE'VE TRIED YOUR WAY BEFORE, HOPHEAD! ONE NEEDLE-FULL OF JOY-JUICE AND YOU GET SO SATISFIED WITH THE WORLD YOU FORGET YOUR OBLIGATIONS! NO, WE'LL DO IT *MY* WAY FOR A CHANGE!

YOU SLIMEY LEECH! I'VE LOST MY HOME, MY WIFE, JOB— *EVERYTHING!* TRADED THEM IN FOR A LOUSY SHOT IN THE ARM! A LITTLE RELIEF FROM THE AGONY THAT SCREAMS FOR MORE AND *MORE!* AND NOW AFTER YOU'VE BLED ME *DRY,* YOU TELL ME....

OKAY! *OKAY!* THERE'S A PACKAGE BEHIND TH' DRESSER— HELP Y'SELF! I'LL SQUARE IT WITH THE *BIG BOSS* SOMEHOW!

YES, *MARY KENNEDY..* YOU TRY TO SQUARE THINGS WITH THE *BIG* BOSS!

P-PUT TH' NEEDLE DOWN!!... *NO!*

OLESON! VOT DAT VAS?? IT SOUND LIKE *JANE!*

BURGLARS MAYBE! YIGGERS! MY *GUN....* AY BANE LEFT IT DOWNSTAIRS!

STOP SHAKING AND GET UP! SHE'S, MAYBE NIGHTMARES HAVING!

GOD BLESS OUR HOME

YOU ALLRIGHT, JANE, YA? NO—LIKE AY SAID, SHE'S DREAMING TINGS AGAIN!! OH, DEAR!

WAIT'LL TONY COMES! HE'LL FIX— DON'T DO IT! I'LL...I'LL....

TCH, TCH!

THUP!

2

TONY! TONY!! HELP!!

NO, IT'S ME—OLIE YOHNSTON! YOUR FRIEND!!— MAMA, YOU TELL HER! YOUR VOICE SHE LIKES!

NO TIME FOR TALKING... TIME FOR GRABBING QUICK BEFORE SHE YUMPS!

??? M-MRS. JOHNSTON! WH-WHAT ARE YOU DOING IN A RACKET LIKE THIS?... OH... ER... SORRY! I THOUGHT—

SUCH DREAMS, YOU POOR TING!...HERE... TIME AY PUT UP CLEAN CURTAINS ANYVAY!.... THAT OLIE!... ONCE HE SAW A MOVIE MAN THROW VATER ON FACE OF GIRL WHO VAS OUT OF HER HEAD—NOW EVERYBODY GETS A BATH

AY TANK AY FIX JANE SOME HOT TEA!

GEE...I MUSTA BEEN PRETTY ROUGH!.. DID I..AH.. SAY ANYTHING?

NOW, YUST FORGET DREAMS AND THIS TONY SOMEBODY! HOT TEA FOR THE NERVES AND YOU BANE SLEEP BETTER, YA?

WH-WHAT'S TH' USE? IT ONLY COMES BACK AN' BACK AN' BACK! -SOB-

JANE, DEAR... EVER SINCE YOU COME TO ROOM HERE, YOU SAY NOTHING, BUT AY SEE! MAYBE NOW YOU LIKE TO TALK?... SOMETIMES IT HELPS, TALKING!

WHEN I THINK OF IT I HAFTA LAUGH! IT WAS GONNA BE SO EASY!.. ALL I HADDA DO WAS CHANGE MY NAME AND ADDRESS AND START OFF FRESH... LEAVE MARY KENNEDY, KANSAS CITY—THE WHOLE MESS— AND WALK AWAY CLEAN!... HAH!! WOULDN'T TONY LOVE TO SEE HIS BROKEN-DOWN MOLL, NOW! YEAH, WE'D BOTH HAVE A GOOD YUK! SOB

THE FEDERAL BUILDING IN KANSAS CITY IS TH' LAST PLACE YA'D EXPECT T'MEET A GANGSTER, IT WAS THAT CRAWLING WITH G-MEN! BUT THEY WERE LIKE NUTHIN' TO TONY PETRILLO! HE USTA BRASS RIGHT INTO PAPA DONNICI'S RESTAURANT, THERE, AN' JUST SIT— NOT SAYIN' A WORD— STARIN' AT ME!! HE'D GET ME SO WEAK IN THE KNEES I COULD HARDLY SERVE...

PAPA, IF YOUR SON CAN WHIP UP FORMULAS LIKE YOU CAN COOK, HE'S A CINCH FOR THE CITY CHEMIST'S SPOT! HOW'S FOR SOME PIE?

MARY, FIXA PIE FOR MIST' INSPECTOR!

AH; JOSEPHI, HE'SA WAN BUSY BOY! YOU SEE HOW MUCH BETTER THE CITY WATER, SHE'SA TASTE SINCE THEY MAKE HIM ASSIST-CHEMIST? AT'SA MY JOE! ALLA TIME HE'SA WORK HARD!

YES, PAPA— OH!... I-I'M SO SORRY!

HERE...LET ME! GEE, HOPE IT DOESN'T LEAVE A SPOT! GUESS I WASN'T WATCHING WHAT I.....I...

THE MAN'SA WAIT FOR HIS PIE, MARY!

3

BUT AS WEEKS WENT BY, I SAW LESS AND LESS OF TONY... AND MORE AND MORE OF HIS "CUSTOMERS"! IT WAS ONE MAD MISERY-GO-ROUND..

DANCE LIKE A CLOUD YE DO!

HI'YA JUICY!

OH, YOU HUNK OF STUFF!!

HUBBA HUBBA!

SWEETSH LIL' GAL INNA WORL'!

MAYBE TOMORROW... MAYBE TONY'LL TAKE ME OUT— MAYBE......

YUM YUM!

AW, C'MON! HAVVA DRINK!

WHERE YA BEEN ALL MY LIFE?

IT WAS ALWAYS THE SAME... WINE AN' DINE... HOME AT TWO..... AND HANG-OVER 'TIL NOON! SURE, THE PAY WAS GOOD, BUT THE PACE WAS KILLIN'!! SWEET LITTLE MARY WAS WILTING!.. FINALLY, ONE NIGHT IT HAPPENED I CRACKED!!...

YOU CAN'T QUIT ME, BABY!.. WHY, YOU'RE MY RIGHT ARM! IF IT'S MORE MONEY YOU WANT—

MONEY! MONEY!! THERE AIN'T ENOUGH IN FORT KNOX TO MAKE ME GO OUT WITH THOSE CRUMS AGAIN! GET SOME OTHER SUCKER TO SET-UP YOUR SALES! I'M THROUGH!!

ALRIGHT, YOU DUMB SAP.. I'M GIVING IT TO YA SQUARE!! DO YOU KNOW WHAT YOUR DATES WERE DOING? — PEDDLING DOPE!! RIGHT UNDER YOUR NOSE! YOU WERE JUST A FRONT!

NO! IT ISN'T TRUE!! YOU'RE LYING JUST TO...

YOU'RE IN IT AS DEEP AS I AM, TOOTS— FOR KEEPS!!

Y-YOU... A...A DOPE DEALER!! AN' I LOVED YOU!! AN' YOU USED IT TO ROPE ME IN!!!.. TONY, HOW COULD YOU?

LOOK...TONY!... LET M-ME GO!.. I WON'T TELL ANYONE!!!! I PROMISE!!! I'LL GO AWAY!... Y-YOU WON'T NEED ME— NOT NOW!! PLEASE!!

IF I WAS IN THE DRIVER'S SEAT MAYBE I WOULD! BUT YOU GOT ME WRONG, KID... I'M JUST A SMALL COG IN THIS RACKET! THE BIG BOSS WOULD EAT US BOTH ALIVE IF YOU TRIED THE REAR EXIT!!

SO LET'S MAKE THE BEST OF IT, KID!.... TELL YOU WHAT.. MAYBE I CAN GET YOU A BETTER SPOT— AT MORE MONEY, TOO!

:SOB: :SOB: YEH, LET'S MAKE LOTSA DOUGH!. THAT'S ALL THAT COUNTS, :SOB: AIN'T IT?

OH, I HATE YOU! HATE YOU!

SOB SOB SOB SOB SOB

A LOTTA FOLKS FEEL TH' SAME WAY, SISTER! WELL, LET'S GET THIS OVER WITH!

WAIT! IF THAT AIN'T OPPORTUNITY KNOCKIN', I NEVER HEARD IT! C'MON!

POUND POUND POUND!

6

ESTHER, IT'S A NATCH!!.. WE'RE TAKIN' OVER CORDOVA ISLAND AND THE DOPE RACKET NEXT WEEK, RIGHT?.. SO WE NAB TONY'S MOLL, AND EASE IT AROUND SHE'S JOINED UP WITH US....

..HE'S SO BURNED, HE FOLLOWS HER TO CORDOVA— AWAY FROM KANSAS CITY... AWAY FROM NOSEY COPS... A NICE QUIET FUNERAL !!

HMMM.. COULD BE! COULD BE!

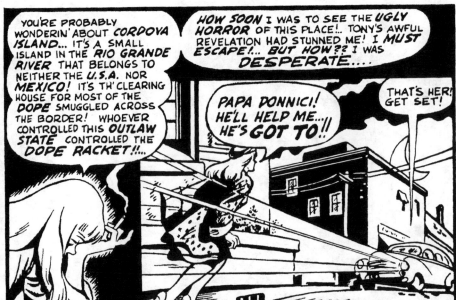

YOU'RE PROBABLY WONDERIN' ABOUT CORDOVA ISLAND... IT'S A SMALL ISLAND IN THE RIO GRANDE RIVER THAT BELONGS TO NEITHER THE U.S.A. NOR MEXICO! IT'S TH' CLEARING HOUSE FOR MOST OF THE DOPE SMUGGLED ACROSS THE BORDER! WHOEVER CONTROLLED THIS OUTLAW STATE CONTROLLED THE DOPE RACKET!!...

HOW SOON I WAS TO SEE THE UGLY HORROR OF THIS PLACE!! TONY'S AWFUL REVELATION HAD STUNNED ME! I MUST ESCAPE!... BUT HOW?? I WAS DESPERATE....

PAPA DONNICI! HE'LL HELP ME.... HE'S GOT TO!!

THAT'S HER! GET SET!

IN YUH GO!

HELP! POLIC!..MMFF!

OKAY, ESTHER!.. NEXT STOP CORDOVA !!

WH-WHAT IS THIS ??.... IF IT'S SOME TRICK OF TONY'S—

RELAX, KID!.. WE WON'T HARM YA! IT'S TONY WHO'S ON TH'SPOT! AND FROM WHERE I SIT, LOOKS LIKE YOU'LL BE GLAD TO HELP US!

R-R-R-R-A

HELP YOU K-KILL TONY?? NO!! NEVER!! OHHH..

I THOUGHT Y'SAID THIS FLUFF HATED TH' GUY?.. THAT SHE'D DO ANYTHING TO GET HIS HIDE ?

BUT SHE SAID IT !! I HEARD A LOT YOU KNOW ABOUT WIMMEN!

WH-WHERE AM I ??

YA BEEN ASLEEP FER HOURS! NOW, BE A GOOD LITTLE GIRL OR —

THERE'S MAXIE'S CAR AHEAD!

OKAY, BOYS! WE JOIN FORCES AND STORM ALL OVER CORDOVA!

EL PASO TEXAS 5 MI

MAXIE, YOU READY?— MAXIE!!! HUBBY!!

HOLY—!! OUR PLAN LEAKED OUT!!

AGH!!

BANG! BANG!

IT'S AN AMBUSH! TO TH' CAR!!

S-SO LONG, HONEY!. SOB I'LL GET 'EM FOR YA.... I'LL KILL 'EM ALL!

7

I DIDN'T DO IT!.. I COULDN'T DO IT!... C-CAN'T YOU SEE WHY?.. I STILL LOVE YA, YA DOG!

NO, GUESS YOU COULDN'T HAVE COOKED IT UP AT THAT. ANY DAME WHO'D FALL FOR ME IS TOO DUMB TO THINK! LET'S GET OUT OF HERE!..IF ESTHER GORDON OR ANY OF HER GOONS ARE STILL AROUND, THIS AIN'T A HEALTHY PLACE TO BE!

WHERE ARE WE GOIN'?

CORDOVA! REMEMBER? --THE ISLAND ESTHER HAD IDEAS ABOUT?... HA, HA! THAT SURE MUST HAVE BEEN A SWELL RECEPTION OUR BOYS HAD FOR HER. THERE'S NOT MUCH GOING ON, THE BIG BOSS AIN'T HEP TO!

HERE WE ARE! STEP ACROSS THIS BRIDGE AND IT'S SAFETY OR DEATH, DEPENDING ON A GUY'S STANDING WITH THE BIG BOSS!

H- HOW DO I STAND, TONY? D-DID HE HEAR THAT RUMOR, TOO?-- ABOUT ME LEAVING YUH?

I WAS JUST COMIN' TO THAT, KID!

...IF HE HASN'T HEARD, OKAY! SWELL! BUT IF HE HAS AND TONY DOESN'T DO SOMETHING ABOUT IT, TONY'S LIFE AIN'T WORTH NUTHIN'!

SNAP!

TONY! YOU BROUGHT ME OUT HERE JUST TO--

THAT'S RIGHT, KID!.. I CAN'T AFFORD TO TAKE... ARG...RISKS...

WHA--?

BANG!

ZING

OUT OF NOWHERE THEY POPPED! TONY'S MEN ON THE ISLAND AND ESTHER GORDON'S REORGANIZED MOB ON THE MAINLAND-- AND TONY AN' ME IN THE MIDDLE--

TAKE 'EM, BOYS! THIS IS FOR MAXIE! BLAST 'EM!

TONY!... F-FOR HEAVEN'S SAKE... TONY!

AGH!

TAT TAT TAT TAT TAT TAT

ZING

9

IF--IF I CAN ONLY GET HIM B-BEHIND...ROCK OUT OF...FIRING LINE...

GROAN

WH-WHY DID YOU DO IT?...I...I WAS GOING...TO KILL YA... YA COULD HAVE..

YOU SAID I WAS DUMB... RECKON THIS PROVES IT-- OH!... G'NIGHT, T-TONY! IT'S -IT'S PAST M-MY BEDTIME...

THEN I WAS DREAMING...OF MURDER AND MOR-PHINE...TONY AND THE BIG BOSS CHASING ME...BEARING DOWN..CLOSER CLOSER...UNTIL..

BANG! YOU'RE DEAD!

EEK!

?? HUH?...WH..?? TONY!...IS THE... SHOOTIN' OVER YET?

HERE'S SOME NEW DUDS! FRESH UP AND MEET ME OUTSIDE! GOT A SURPRISE!

HA, HA! HOURS AGO! ESTHER'S GOONS ARE LAYING ALL OVER THE LANDSCAPE! IT WAS A ROUTE!...AND--OH, YES-- THE BIG BOSS DIDN'T HEAR THAT RUMOR! YOU'RE IN THE CLEAR WITH HIM--AND ME AFTER LAST NIGHT!

REMEMBER THAT NEW JOB I PROMISED YOU, MARY? HERE IT IS...MEET THE PROFESSOR!

HOW'JA DO?

I WON'T BE SEEING YOU FOR AWHILE, KID-- GOT BUSINESS IN K.C.! BUT YOU'RE IN GOOD HANDS!

MY, YOU'RE QUITE A DIFFERENT LOOKING GIRL THAN THE POOR CREATURE OF LAST NIGHT!

CORDOVA ISLAND IS THE NUCLEUS OF A VAST ORGAN-IZATION, MISS KENNEDY... AND NATURALLY, IT REQUIRES A LOT OF BOOKKEEPING-- WHICH SHALL BE YOUR DUTY!

NOW, HERE IS OUR-- ER..DRUGSTORE! YOU WILL KEEP RECORDS OF ALL INCOMING AND OUTGOING SHIP-MENTS!

THEN, TOO, THE MAINTENANCE OF SUCH A STRONG HOUSEHOLD REQUIRES QUITE A CROUCHING ARMY! THERE WILL BE PAY-ROLLS TO MEET!

10

YOU'LL HAVE A TIME KEEPING UP WITH OUR EVER-CHANGING PERSONNEL AT FIRST. WE JUST CAN'T SEEM TO KEEP *HELP ON CORDOVA!* IF IT ISN'T WAR CASUALTIES, IT'S THE DOPE RUNNERS-- ALWAYS TRYING TO STEAL OUR GOODS-- DISCOURAGING ISN'T IT?

YOU'RE QUIET, MISS KENNEDY! THINKING PERHAPS?

(UGH)... H-HOW DO YOU GET AWAY WITH IT? I MEAN THE LAW-- DON'T THE AUTHORITIES GIVE YOU TROUBLE?

THE BIG BOSS IS THE LAW HERE! THIS IS AN INDEPENDENT ISLAND! NEITHER UNCLE SAM NOR MEXICO CAN TOUCH US! HERE A MAN CAN MURDER AND *BE MURDERED* WITHOUT FEAR OF PROSECUTION! WELL! I'VE TALKED ENOUGH! READY FOR WORK, MISS KENNEDY?

EH?... I-I GUESS SO!

AND I LEFT A GOOD JOB DANCING WITH DERELICTS FOR THIS!

EVERY MINUTE ON THAT COFFIN-ISLE DROVE ME ANOTHER PEG INTO MY HOPELESS DESPAIR... I WAS LOST! A FROG HAS A *HAIR-LIKE* CHANCE TO ESCAPE THE *BIG BOSS* WHOEVER HE WAS! THE ONLY HALF-WAY CIVIL PERSON THERE WAS THE PROF! FINALLY AFTER WEEKS THERE, HE--

PACK YOUR LIPSTICK, MISS KENNEDY... JUST GOT ORDERS TO TAKE YOU BACK TO KANSAS CITY. ANOTHER PROMOTION FOR YOU!

GOLLY, DO YOU MEAN--?(ULP) ER-- YES, PROFESSOR!

AND SO, WE RELUCTANTLY BID LEAVE TO THE ENCHANTING ISLE OF THE DEAD, MISS KENNEDY. WHATEVER SIDETRACKED YOU INTO A RACKET LIKE THIS?

LOOK WHO'S ASKING! YOU WITH *HARVARD* POURIN' OUT YOUR MOUTH: THE *POT* CALLS THE *KETTLE* BLACK!

ME, I'M IN IT FOR *WHAT OTHER REASON IS THERE? COLD CASH... AND I LOVE IT-- SEE?*

WHO ARE YOU ATTEMPTING TO CONVINCE, ME-- OR OH, WELL...

YOU WILL RELAY SHIPMENTS DIRECTLY FROM YOUR APARTMENT, MISS KENNEDY. TONY WILL INSTRUCT YOU FURTHER. ...AND DON'T FORGET IF YOU EVER NEED ANY HELP.

SURE! I'LL RUN *RIGHT TO YOU* THE MIN MY *ELECTRIC DISHWASHER* GOES ON THE FRITZ! GOOD BYE, MR. WHISKERS!

OH, HOW I WANTED TO POUR MYSELF OUT TO HIM-- TO TELL HIM THE *TRUTH!*... BUT THE GUY WAS *TOO SMOOTH!* SUPPOSING HE WAS JUST *TESTING* ME? MAYBE HE WAS THE *BIG BOSS* HIMSELF? ANYWAY, I WASN'T WORKING WITH TONY LONG WHEN *ANOTHER* JOLT CAME--

HALLO, JOSEPH! HOW'S THE BUDDING CHEMIST THESE DAYS? PAPA DONNICI TELLS ME--

HA! YOU KNOW DAD, ED! WHATEVER HE SAYS I'M DOING, IT'S HALF THAT GOOD!

WAIT'LL HE GETS A LITTLE FURTHER DOWN.

11

MIO DIO! IT'S PAPA DONNICI'S BOY! *GLG!*

GOOD HEAVENS! IT CAN'T BE!

DAILY EXPRES
CITY CHEMIST
JOSEPH DONNICI KILLED BY GANGSTERS!

BELIEVED VICTIM OF MISTAKEN IDENTITY

PAPA! IT'S ME-- MARY!... I JUST HEARD THE HORRIBLE NEWS... WHY, YOU POOR DEAR! YOU SHOULDN'T HAVE TO DO THAT NOW! GIVE ME YOUR APRON!

IT'SA HOKAY, MARY... SOB... I DO SOMETING OR I GO *CRAZY!* SOB...SOB...SOB... WHO JOEY HARM? GERMS MAYBE... NOBODY ELSE... SOB...SOB...

DA PAPER SHE'SA SAY MY JOEY SHOT BY MISTAKE!...SOB...SOB... PLEESA EXCUSE... SO SORRY! IT'SA ALL RIGHT-- I GOT *LOTSA* JOEY'S! HE'SA GROW ON *TREES!* SOB...

PAPA, I--

ALLA TIME HE'SA ASK 'BOUT YOU, MARY! "HOW'S MARY'S NEW LOTSA MONEY JOB," HE SAY!...LONGA TIME YOU NO COME SEE US...*SNIFF*.. I TELL HIM YOU ONE BUSY GIRL AND HAPPY, YES?

EVERYTHING'S FINE, PAPA! JUST D-DANDY! IF THERE'S ANYTHING I CAN DO FOR YOU...

I. I COULDN'T TELL PAPA THE *TRUTH!* WHAT IF IT WAS TONY'S MOB --*MY* MOB-- WHO KILLED JOE? OH, GLORY, IF IT WAS... IF SOMETHING DOESN'T BREAK SOON, I'LL *DIE!*

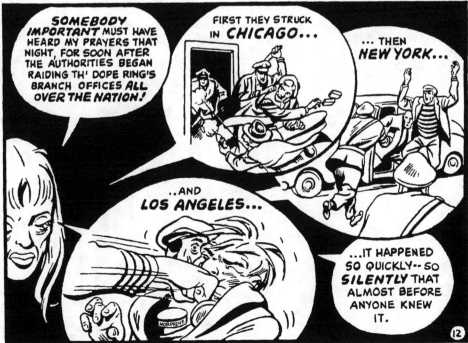

SOMEBODY *IMPORTANT* MUST HAVE HEARD MY PRAYERS THAT NIGHT, FOR SOON AFTER THE AUTHORITIES BEGAN RAIDING TH' DOPE RING'S BRANCH OFFICES *ALL OVER THE NATION!*

FIRST THEY STRUCK IN *CHICAGO...*

... THEN *NEW YORK...*

..AND *LOS ANGELES...*

...IT HAPPENED SO QUICKLY-- SO *SILENTLY* THAT ALMOST BEFORE ANYONE KNEW IT.

12

13

HERE'S WHAT YOU SHOULDA HAD LONG AGO-- D*X!! YOU!

TO-GASP-NY!

GET HIM, MAC!

YOU, TOO, COPPERS! I'LL KILL-- KILL...

H-HONEST, TONY... YOU KNOW... HOW IT IS... WITH ME...

HE'S DEAD, MISS KENNEDY...THE MAN YOU LOVED--WHO WOULD HAVE KILLED YOU! YOU NEEDN'T BE AFRAID NOW! WE HAVE ALL THE OTHERS IN CUSTODY!

PERHAPS NOW YOU'LL BE WILLING TO COOPERATE WITH THE AUTHORITIES!

Y-YOU KNOW WHO THE BIG BOSS IS?

THAT'S WHY I JOINED THE GANG-- TO FIND OUT! BUT THE REAL TIP-OFF WAS THE KILLING OF JOSEPH DONNIC!! WE FOUND THAT WAS NO ACCIDENT, MISS KENNEDY! IT WAS ESTHER GORDON'S REVENGE AGAINST THE BIG BOSS, WHO WAS--

PAPA DONNICI! NO! NO!

HE WAS MY FRIEND!! EVERYBODY'S FRIEND! HOW MANY TIMES I NEARLY WENT TO HIM FOR HELP!.. AND ALL THE WHILE HE-- HE -- OH, GEEZE... AIN'T THERE ANYONE IN THE WORLD YA CAN TRUST??

IF I LIVE A MILLION YEARS, I'LL NEVER F'GET IT!... PAPA DONNICI...! I TURNED STATES WITNESS AND HELPED SEND HIM AND HIS SLIMEY CREW UP THE RIVER! ME?.. I GOT THE LONGEST SENTENCE OF ALL--THREE MONTHS IN JAIL AND A LIFE TIME OF REGRET! I'LL NEVER BE FREE!

JANE-- ER, MARY! YOU KNOW WHAT BY TANK?

TELL YOUR STORY, TO THE WORLD!....JUST THE WAY YOU TELL IT TO ME! MAYBE YOU BANE HELP KEEP OTHER FOOLISH GIRLS FROM MAKING SAME MISTAKE-- MAYBE THEN YOU FEEL BETTER, YA?

IF-- IF ONLY I COULD! OH. DEAR SWEET MRS. JOHNSTON! I LOVE YOU! I LOVE YOU! AND BELIEVE ME, HERE'S A GIRL WHO REALLY KNOWS NOW WHAT LOVE IS!

SO THAT'S IT-- JUST AS MRS. JOHNSTON GOT IT. MEBBE NOW I CAN SLEEP...MEBBE NOT... BUT IF MY STORY CAN SHOW SOME UNTHINKING SOULS THE FOOLISH FOLLY OF CRIME, I RECKON IT'LL BE WORTH IT.' Y'UNNERSTAND?

14

"I WAS A COME-ON GIRL FOR BROKEN BONES, INC."

QUIT STRUGGLING, MISTER! -- YOU KNEW WHAT YOU WERE IN FOR WHEN KITTY BROUGHT YOU UP HERE!

SOMETIME AROUND 1932, IN UPSTATE NEW YORK, A GROUP OF DISTINGUISHED CITIZENS WERE OPERATING A SCHEME TO EXTRACT PAYMENTS FROM INSURANCE COMPANIES --- THEIR OPERATIONS, WHEN UNCOVERED, SHOCKED THE ENTIRE CIVILIZED WORLD! HERE, FOR THE FIRST TIME, IS AN EYEWITNESS ACCOUNT OF THEIR DIABOLICAL OPERATIONS!

EXPOSING THE BRUTAL ACCIDENT-INSURANCE RACKET!

FOOL-PROOF OPPORTUNITY TO EARN BIG MONEY FOR RIGHT PERSON OF EXECUTIVE TYPE. NO INVESTMENT....

- OFFICES -

"WHEN I SAW THE AD, I DIDN'T THINK TOO SERIOUSLY OF IT, BUT MARKED IT WITH MY PENCIL BECAUSE IT SOMEHOW HELD MY INTEREST... I WAS JUST KITTY CRAMER, A FRESH KID OUT OF COLLEGE --- AND A LITTLE TOO AMBITIOUS!!!

NO INVESTMENT-- --HMM --WELL WHAT HAVE I GOT TO LOSE? I'LL ANSWER THE AD...

"I DID ANSWER, AND MUCH TO MY SURPRISE, A FEW DAYS LATER, I RECEIVED A PHONE CALL!"

YES, THIS IS KITTY CRAMER! OH, THE ADVERTISEMENT! WHY, CERTAINLY I'LL ANSWER A FEW QUESTIONS!

WHAT WOULD YOU LIKE TO KNOW, MISTER NICHOLS?

ARE YOU LOOKING FOR SOME *PARTICULAR* TYPE OF POSITION, MISS CRAMER? OR ARE YOU INTERESTED IN ANYTHING — TO MAKE *MONEY*?

"I TOLD YOU I WAS A FRESH KID--AND I THOUGHT THEN THAT I WAS SMART TOO! -- *WHAT A CHUMP I WAS!*"

LOOK, MISTER-- YOUR AD SAID YOU HAD A BUSINESS DEAL! IF IT'S AN EXECUTIVE JOB, I'LL BE PERFECT FOR IT!

"SURE, I KNEW IT WAS SOME KIND OF A RACKET, BUT I WANTED TO FIND OUT HOW CROOKED IT WAS! SO WE MADE AN APPOINTMENT---I SHOWED UP..."

J. NICHOLS

INVESTMENTS

"J. NICHOLS, INVESTMENTS" WELL, MISTER NICHOLS, LET'S SEE WHAT YOU HAVE TO OFFER LITTLE KITTY?

AHH—MISS KRAMER! COME RIGHT IN! I'M JAMES NICHOLS!

THANK YOU!

I'LL GET TO THE POINT, MISS CRAMER! I THINK I KNOW THE RIGHT PERSON WHEN I SEE HER... I PRIDE MYSELF ON BEING A GOOD JUDGE OF CHARACTER—

QUIT STALLING, NICHOLS! JUST HOW SHADY *IS* YOUR DEAL!

2

3

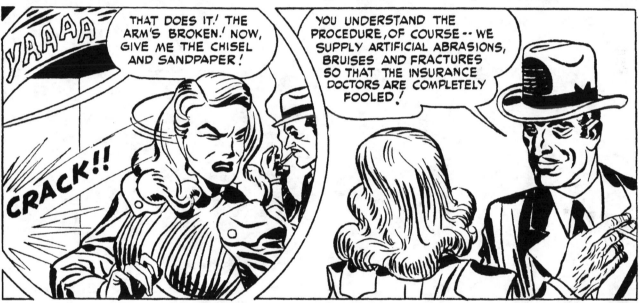

5

GOOD HEAVENS! HE'S -- HE'S *DEAD!*

NICHOLS-- --IT'S-- *MURDER!*

HIS HEART WOULDN'T STAND THE PAIN!! I *TOLD* YOU -- I TOLD-A-AAA--

YOU'RE GETTING HYSTERICAL, KITTY! SHUT UP AND PULL YOURSELF TOGETHER!

SLAP--

KITTY WAS RIGHT, NICHOLS! I KNEW WE SHOULD'VE TURNED THE OLD GEEZER DOWN!

QUIET, YOU QUACK! WE DON'T *HAVE* TO GET MIXED UP IN THIS! GIVE ME A HAND WITH THIS STIFF!

"NICHOLS HAD NERVE, ALL RIGHT! HE AND DOC FIXED IT SO THE POOR, OLD GUY WOULD LOOK LIKE A HIT-AND-RUN VICTIM...

THAT'S IT! LAY HIM DOWN HERE IN THE CENTER OF THE ROAD...IT'S A PERFECT SETUP!

NOW, WE'LL SCRAPE UP THE SURFACE OF THE ROAD NEAR THOSE TIRE TRACKS SO IT WILL LOOK LIKE THE OLD GENT BOUNCED AROUND A BIT!

NOTHING LIKE BEING REALISTIC, EH, NICHOLS?

"AS FOR ME, I WASN'T THE FRESH COLLEGE KID NOW --- I WAS *SCARED* -- AND SCARED SILLY!

I CAN'T STAND THE THOUGHT OF THAT OLD MAN'S FACE -- AND NICHOLS -- HE WON'T STOP WITH THIS ONE ---

7

ALL NAMES IN THIS STORY ARE FICTICIOUS

STELLA MAE DICKSON...
The BOBBY SOX BANDIT QUEEN

THE FIRST ONE WHO MAKES A MOVE WHILE MY HUSBAND RIFLES THE VAULT, GETS A *BULLET* BETWEEN THE EYES! GET ME?

THE AMAZING, *TRUE* STORY OF A TEEN-AGE GIRL WHO TERRORIZED THE NATION! -- UNTIL THE *FBI* STEPPED IN!

NOT ALL NOTORIOUS CRIMINALS ARE CAPTURED IN SENSATIONAL AND DRAMATIC FASHION.... MANY FRONT PAGE ARRESTS ATTRACT LITTLE ATTENTION - EVEN WHEN THEY OCCUR IN FULL VIEW OF THE PUBLIC...

IT WAS EARLY EVENING IN KANSAS CITY ON APRIL 7, 1939...THE OBJECT OF CHUCK'S OBSERVANT EYE WAS A BEAUTIFUL, TEEN-AGE GIRL WHO DIDN'T SEEM AT ALL DIFFERENT FROM ANY OTHER OF HER BOBBY-SOX SISTERS!

S'MATTER, CHUCK, AIN'TCHA TAKIN' A CHICK OUT TONIGHT?

COULD BE, HARRY-- *SAY*-- LOOK OVER THERE, WILLYA?

BOY, WHAT A NUMBER *SHE* IS!

Y'KNOW, HARRY, MAYBE I *WILL* BE TAKIN' A CHICK OUT TONIGHT AT THAT!

READ THE EVENING POST 5¢

BUT AS THE GIRL APPROACHED THE STREET CORNER, TWO MEN EMERGED FROM A CAR PARKED NEAR THE CURB TO ENGAGE THE GIRL IN CONVERSATION!

LOOKS LIKE YOU'RE TOO LATE, CHUCK!

WELL, HOW DO YA LIKE *THAT* FOR A BREAK?

YA CAN'T WORK FAST ENOUGH FOR GOOD LOOKERS, CHUCK! THERE'S ALWAYS TWO OTHER GUYS AHEAD OF YA!!

THIS CERTAINLY PROVES YOU'RE RIGHT, HARRY! SHE'S GETTING IN THE CAR WITH THEM! OH, WELL---

THERE SHE GOES! GOSH, IF I'D ONLY BEEN A LITTLE QUICKER ON THE UPTAKE!

DON'T BAWL, CHUCK! THESE GUYS MUST'VE BEEN WAITIN' FOR HER! SHE PROBABLY HAD A DATE WITH 'EM!

ZOOM-

HARRY *WAS RIGHT*, IN A WAY... THE MEN *HAD* BEEN WAITING FOR THE GIRL-- BUT THEY WERE F.B.I. AGENTS! FOR THE GIRL *DID* HAVE A DATE-- BUT IT WAS WITH JUSTICE! CHUCK AND HARRY WERE UNAWARE THAT THEY HAD WITNESSED ONE OF THE MOST WIDELY DISCUSSED INCIDENTS OF 1939-- THE CAPTURE OF STELLA MAE DICKSON, *THE BOBBY-SOX BANDIT QUEEN!!!*

GETCHA PAPER! READ ALL ABOUT IT! G-MEN CAPTURE STELLA MAE DICKSON! *EXTRY!*

YOUTHFUL PUBLIC ENEMY TAKEN INTO CUSTODY BY F.B.I.

YES, THIS UNSPECTACULAR ACTION BY THE F.B.I HAD BROUGHT TO AN END ONE OF THE MOST AMAZING CAREERS IN CRIMINAL HISTORY...THIS 17 YEAR OLD GIRL, HARDLY MORE THAN AN ADOLESCENT, WAS CONSIDERED AS *DANGEROUS AND DESTRUCTIVE* AS THE MOST HARDENED OF THE NATION'S PUBLIC ENEMIES!!

STELLA'S FANTASTIC STORY BEGAN IN A ROLLER SKATING RINK IN THE SUMMER OF 1937, WHEN SHE WAS JUST STELLA MAE IRWIN AND ONLY 15 YEARS OLD...

SAY, YOU'RE GREAT WITH THOSE SKATES! HOW ABOUT A FEW FANCY TURNS TOGETHER? THE NAME'S BENNY DICKSON!

OKAY! I DON'T SEE WHY NOT-- IT MIGHT BE FUN!

2

AN EVIL STAR MUST HAVE SHONE BRIGHTLY THAT NIGHT... BENNY DICKSON AND STELLA IRWIN HAD FOUND EACH OTHER.!! BEING MUTUAL TYPES, THEY FOUND THEMSELVES IN A WHIRLWIND ROMANCE!

GOSH, I WISH THIS PLACE WOULDN'T CLOSE SO EARLY! I COULD SKATE UNTIL MORNING!

LIKED IT, EH, KID?

MIND IF I SEE YOU HOME, BABY? I'VE GOT MY BUS OUTSIDE... WHAT DO YOU SAY?

I LIKE YOU, BENNY! YOU'RE DIFFERENT FROM MOST FELLOWS I KNOW... YOU'RE GOOD COMPANY! SHALL WE GO?

BENNY WAS DIFFERENT--AND STELLA SOON FOUND OUT WHY, FROM HIS OWN LIPS...

HOW DO YOU LIKE THIS NEW CAR, BABY? I GOT IT FOR THE ANNIVERSARY OF OUR FIFTH DATE TOGETHER!

THIS IS AN AWFULLY EXPENSIVE CAR, BENNY! HOW CAN YOU AFFORD IT?

LISTEN, BABY--A SMART OPERATOR CAN GET ANYTHING HE WANTS.. SNATCHING THIS CONVERTIBLE WAS ONLY A LITTLE THING COMPARED TO WHAT I COULD GET FOR YOU!

BENNY! YOU MEAN YOU STOLE THIS CAR?

DON'T ACT SURPRISED, BABY! YOU'RE THRILLED AND YOU KNOW IT! YOU'RE JUST LIKE ME! YOU WANT MONEY, CLOTHES AND EXCITEMENT! -- WELL, STICK WITH LITTLE BENNY -- I'LL SHOW YOU HOW TO GET ALL THAT THE EASY WAY!

BUT, BENNY, AREN'T YOU AFRAID OF THE POLICE?

I'M TOO SMART FOR 'EM, I TELL YA! ALWAYS A STEP AHEAD! I'M NO AMATEUR! I'VE SERVED TIME IN THE PEN... I KNOW THE ROPES!

3

IT WASN'T LONG BEFORE STELLA WAS 'GOING STEADY' WITH 27 YEAR - OLD BENNY ---

STELLA, I GOTTA BLOW TOWN FAST! AS SOON AS I'M SET UP I'LL SEND FOR YOU!

MAKE IT SOON, BENNY! I'M GOING TO MISS YOU!

NOT LONG AFTER, STELLA JOINED BENNY IN CALIFORNIA!!

IT'S SO NICE BEING WITH YOU AGAIN, BENNIE!

IT'S GREAT TO SEE YOU, BABY! COME ON, WE'RE GOING TO GET HITCHED FIRST THING!

IMAGINE THAT CALIFORNIA JUDGE SAYING YOU WERE TOO YOUNG TO BE MARRIED? WELL, WE'LL HEAD FOR MY PARENTS' SUMMER HOME IN MINNESOTA AND GET SPLICED AS SOON AS WE ARRIVE!

BENNY DID MARRY STELLA IN HIS PARENTS' HOME...HIS FATHER, A HIGH SCHOOL TEACHER, OFFERED BENNY THE OPPORTUNITY TO STUDY-- BUT YOUNG DICKSON POSSESSED A RESTLESS SPIRIT!

AHH- THIS STUDYING BUSINESS IS PRETTY DULL! IT BORES ME STIFF!

FORGET THAT OLD BOOK AND GIVE BABY A GREAT, BIG KISS!

Y'KNOW, BENNY, THIS PLACE IS AWFULLY QUIET! I'M GETTING TO FEEL LIKE I'M BURIED ALIVE!

SAY I'VE GOT AN IDEA TO BREAK THE MONOTONY! WHAT DO YOU SAY TO SOME TARGET PRACTICE?

YOU MEAN SHOOTING-- WITH GUNS?

SURE! I'LL MAKE AN ANNIE OAKLEY OF YOU IN NO TIME AT ALL!

4

WHERE ARE YOU CHILDREN OFF TO?

WE'RE GOING TO DO A LITTLE HUNTING, POP! STELLA AND I COULD USE SOME FRESH AIR!

BUT INSTEAD OF HUNTING, BENNY TAUGHT STELLA THE USE OF FIRE ARMS! AND STELLA BROUGHT REALITY TO BENNY'S PREDICTION! SHE PROVED TO *BE* AN ANNIE OAKLEY -- A DEAD SHOT WITH A GUN!

THERE'S SIX BULL'S EYES!

GOOD SHOOTING, STELLA! NOW LET'S SEE WHAT YOU CAN DO WITH THE RIFLE!

BAM!

WOW! ALL OF THEM -- *DEAD CENTER!* YOU'RE A NATURAL, BABY!

YOU'VE GOT *TALENT,* BABY! -- *REAL* TALENT! AND LITTLE BENNY'S GOING TO PLAN BIG THING FOR US BOTH!

OH, BENNY! I'M SO THRILLED!

BENNY WASN'T KIDDING! HE BEGAN FORMULATING PLANS ALMOST AT ONCE... IT WASN'T LONG BEFORE HE TOLD STELLA ABOUT THEM!

BABY, I'VE LINED UP THAT LITTLE BANK IN ELKTON, SOUTH DAKOTA! THINK YOU'RE READY FOR A CRACK AT IT?

SURE, BENNY! THAT WOULD BE FUN! BUT AREN'T YOU AFRAID, WITH THE POLICE RECORD YOU HAVE?

I LEARNED ALL THE ANGLES WHILE DOING TIME IN THE MISSOURI PEN, KID! WE WON'T MISS!

OKAY, BENNY! WHAT DO YOU WANT ME TO DO?

5

ON AUGUST 25, 1938, THE DAY BEFORE STELLA'S 16TH BIRTHDAY, SHE SET OFF, DISGUISED IN MALE ATTIRE, WITH HER HUSBAND TO TAKE PART IN HER FIRST CRIME!

WAIT HERE, BABY! I'LL BE RIGHT OUT!

BE CAREFUL, BENNY!

THIS IS A STICKUP! OPEN YOUR VAULT AND GET THAT DOUGH OUT!

WE CAN'T! THE VAULTS ON A TIME LOCK AND WON'T OPEN FOR ANOTHER HALF HOUR!

THAT'S ALRIGHT, I'LL WAIT! BUT THE FIRST ONE WHO TRIES ANY TRICKS GETS HURT--- BAD!

STELLA BECAME WORRIED WHEN BENNY DIDN'T RE-APPEAR ON TIME... SHE DECIDED TO CHECK ON THE SITUATION!

BENNY, WHAT'S WRONG!

GOTTA WAIT FOR THE TIME LOCK...HELP ME COVER THESE FISH!

THE BANDITS WAITED THIRTY MINUTES! AS NEW PATRONS CAME IN, THEY WERE ADDED TO THE GROWING GROUP OF PRISONERS!

THE VAULT'S OPEN! KEEP 'EM COVERED WHILE I CLEAN HOUSE!

OKAY! ALL OF YOU-- GET INSIDE THE VAULT, QUICK!

YOU HEARD WHAT HE SAID! GET MOVING!

6

FOOLHARDY AS THEIR 30 MINUTES DELAY SEEMED, BENNY AND STELLA ESCAPED ARREST AND MADE THEIR GETAWAY TO A FARM IN MINNESOTA BELONGING TO A RELATIVE OF BENNY'S! THE ROBBERY VICTIMS WERE LATER RESCUED FROM THE VAULT WHERE THEY ALMOST SUFFOCATED!!

HOW DID WE DO?

NOT TOO WELL, BABY! TWO THOUSAND, ONE HUNDRED SEVENTY FOUR DOLLARS AND SIXTY FOUR CENTS!

MEANWHILE, BENNY AND STELLA WENT TO DETROIT! BENNY BOUGHT A CAR AND STELLA, SOME NEW CLOTHES! ON THEIR WAY BACK, BENNY COMPLETELY WRECKED THE NEW SEDAN NEAR OSAGE CITY!

THE CAR'S OUT OF CONTROL! LOOK OUT!

CRASH!

THE DICKSONS WERE INACTIVE FOR AWHILE ...THEN, ON THE MORNING OF OCTOBER 31, 1938, THEY APPEARED IN BROOKINGS, SOUTH DAKOTA!

NOW, BABY!

GOOD! HE'S JUST OPENING THE BANK!

BUT THE ROBBED BANK HAD BEEN INSURED BY THE "FEDERAL DEPOSIT INSURANCE CO."-- WHICH BROUGHT THE CRIME TO THE ATTENTION OF THE *F.B.I.*! BENNY AND STELLA HAD COMMITTED A FEDERAL OFFENSE!

YOU CAN REST ASSURED, SIR, THAT WE'LL HAVE THOSE TWO IN CUSTODY IN GOOD TIME! OUR AGENTS ARE ALREADY AT WORK ON THE CASE!

THE LUCKY PAIR MIRACULOUSLY ESCAPED WITH THEIR LIVES! HOWEVER, BENNY AND STELLA SOON HAD ANOTHER CAR! THEY STOLE IT IN KANSAS CITY!!

SAY, THIS BUS RUNS SMOOTHER THAN OUR *LAST* CAR, BABY!

BETTER KEEP YOUR EYE ON THE ROAD, OR IT'LL END UP THE SAME WAY, BENNY!

INTO THE BACK OF THE BANK, POP! NO PEEPS NOW OR I'LL CROAK YOU!

I'LL STAY HERE AND NAIL THE OTHER CLERKS AS THEY COME IN!

7

WHEN THE LAST CLERK TO REPORT FOR WORK ENTERED THE BANK, HE JOINED THE OTHERS--- UNDER THE STEADY MUZZLE OF STELLA'S GUN!

HERE'S THE LAST ONE, BENNY!

SWELL! I PICKED UP *TWO GRAND* RIFLING THESE CAGES!

BUT THIS IS SMALL CHANGE! WHEN DOES THE *VAULT* OPEN, MISTER?

T-TEN THIRTY--

TEN THIRTY! BENNY KNEW BUSINESS WOULD BE IN FULL SWING THEN...HE THOUGHT FAST!!

LISTEN, YOU BANK CLERKS! I'M GONNA LET YOU DO A LITTLE HONEST WORK! GET IN YOUR CAGES AND TAKE CARE OF THE CUSTOMERS WHEN THEY COME IN! I'LL EVEN *LEND* YOU A FEW HUNDRED FOR PETTY CASH!

I CUT THE WIRES IN THE JOINT SO DON'T TRY TO CALL FOR HELP...AND KEEP YOUR NOSES CLEAN WITH THE TRADE! JUST REMEMBER--WE'RE *BOTH DEAD SHOTS!*

NONE OF THE FORTY DEPOSITORS THAT MORNING BECAME SUSPICIOUS...FINALLY, 10:30 ARRIVED AND THE VAULT DOOR SLOWLY SWUNG OPEN....

TEN THIRTY! BENNY SHOULD BE IN THE VAULT BY NOW! HAH! IF THESE YOKELS ONLY KNEW A ROBBERY IS GOING ON UNDER THEIR VERY NOSES!

GET ANOTHER GUY AND CARRY THIS SWAG OUT TO THE CAR!

8

TAKE THESE GUYS AND THE DOUGH OUT TO THE CAR! I'LL BE ALONG IN A SECOND!

BEFORE BENNY JOINED STELLA AND THEIR HOSTAGES, HE CASUALLY STROLLED TOWARD A TELLER'S CAGE AND LEFT A FINAL FRIGHTENING ORDER!

WE'RE TAKING TWO OF YOUR MEN *WITH* US! SO, IF ANYONE SQUAWKS BEFORE WE GET AWAY-- I'LL KILL THEM BOTH! SO LONG ---

THE BANDITS ONCE MORE MADE A CLEAN GET-AWAY!

BETTER *DUMP* THOSE TWO CHARACTERS, STELLA! WE'RE NOWHERE NEAR A TELEPHONE!

THE POLICE WILL GET YOU RATS YET! YOU WON'T GET AWAY WITH THIS!

HA-HA-HA-HA- WHAT A SWEET JOB *THAT* WAS, BENNY! IT WENT LIKE CLOCKWORK!

BENNY AND STELLA GOT AWAY WITH ALMOST $50,000! DURING THE MONTH THAT FOLLOWED THEY LIVED IN GRAND STYLE! ON THANKSGIVING DAY, THEY WERE PREPARING TO LEAVE A TOURIST CABIN WHERE THEY HAD MADE A BRIEF STOP...

THE LOCAL COPS GOT A LEAD THROUGH THAT HOT CAR I DITCHED!

WE'D BETTER MOVE FAST, THEN!

THERE HE IS! THAT'S DICKSON!

DICKSON! STOP! YOU'RE UNDER ARREST!

YOU'LL HAVE TO *CATCH* ME FIRST, COPPER!

9

THE SIDE OF STELLA'S HEAD WAS BLEEDING PROFUSELY, BUT WITH UNERRING AIM SHE BLASTED AWAY AT THE PURSUING CAR WITH HER RIFLE!!!

THE DICKSONS DECIDED TO ABANDON THEIR CAR AND APPROPRIATE A NEW ONE FROM THE FIRST PASSERBY UNLUCKY ENOUGH TO CROSS THEIR PATH.!!

AT DAYBREAK, THE DICKSONS FOUND THEY NEEDED A FASTER CAR! THEY GOT ONE BY USING THEIR USUAL NEFARIOUS METHOD!

LATE THAT NIGHT, BENNY AND STELLA RACED ALONG THE HIGHWAY IN THE NEIGHBOR'S CAR, TAKING THE TWO FARMERS ALONG TO KEEP THE ALARM FROM SPREADING!!

WHEN IT WAS CONSIDERED SAFE, THE OUTLAWS ROUGHLY DUMPED THEIR HOSTAGES ON THE ROAD..THE DICKSONS LATER LEFT THE STOLEN CAR AND BOUGHT AN OLD, SECOND HAND MODEL!

THE G-MEN WILL NEVER FIND US HERE IN NEW ORLEANS, WILL THEY, BENNY?

AAAH! THEY'RE PROBABLY RUNNING IN *CIRCLES* FOLLOWIN' CRUMMY LEADS, BABY! HA! HA! HA! HA!

BENNY WAS RIGHT! THE F.B.I. WASN'T IDLE! THEY WERE TRACKING DOWN EVERY LEAD THAT PRESENTED ITSELF!-- IN ANY PART OF THE NATION!--*IN CALIFORNIA!*

HOW LONG DID THEY STAY HERE?

WHY, JUST A FEW DAYS, IF I REMEMBER RIGHT!

---IN MINNESOTA--

WHEN DID THEY LEAVE?

OH, I'D SAY ABOUT A WEEK AFTER THEY CAME HERE--

--IN KANSAS--

DID YOU KNOW STELLA MAE IRWIN?

YES, BUT I DON'T KNOW WHERE SHE IS NOW! ARE YOU ONE OF HER OLD BOY FRIEND?

--IN SOUTH DAKOTA---

THAT WAS ON OCTOBER THIRTY FIRST?

YES! ONE OF MY BANK CLERKS AND MYSELF WERE THROWN OUT ON THE ROAD BY THEM AFTER THEY WERE WELL OUT OF TOWN!

AND IN INDIANA---

THEN WHAT HAPPENED?

CAN'T RIGHTLY SAY, MISTER! I SAW THE CAR TEAR PLUMB CRAZY-LIKE TOWARD THE HIGHWAY!

12

THE F.B.I. INVESTIGATION WAS THOROUGH! NO DETAIL WAS OVERLOOKED! THE TRAIL OF THE DICKSONS WAS CLEAR NOW... THE G-MEN WERE READY TO CLOSE IN!

THE NOTE FOUND IN THE GROCERIES WAS A MESSAGE FROM BENNY DICKSON ARRANGING A MEETING WITH A PAL... IT BECAME, INSTEAD, A RENDEZVOUS WITH JUSTICE!!!

YEP! HERE IT IS-- IN THIS BAG OF PEARS! WHERE DID YOU GET THIS, LITTLE GIRL?

A PRETTY YOUNG LADY WITH YELLOW HAIR PAID ME TO DELIVER THESE GROCERIES!

STELLA MAE DICKSON!

IT'S DICKSON! CAREFUL! HE'S DANGEROUS!

LET'S GET HIM!

ALRIGHT, DICKSON, WE'RE F.B.I.! LET'S GO!

DON'T TRY ANYTHING YOU'LL BE SORRY FOR!

YOU'LL STOP LEAD BEFORE YOU TAKE ME IN!

WHY, YOU DUMB THUG!

A-A-A-A-A-A—

STELLA WAS IN A NEARBY CAR AND SAW BENNY DIE! SHE QUICKLY DROVE OFF AND LATER ABANDONED THE VEHICLE TO CATCH A BUS TO KANSAS CITY!! BUT THE G-MEN WERE RIGHT BEHIND HER... STELLA, UNLIKE BENNY, WENT QUIETLY... HER SPREE OF VIOLENCE WAS OVER!

STELLA MAE DICKSON, YOU'VE BEEN FOUND GUILTY AS CHARGED!

TEN YEARS IN PRISON WAS STELLA'S SENTENCE! THAT WAS ON AUGUST 21, 1939, JUST FIVE DAYS BEFORE SHE REACHED SEVENTEEN!--A YOUNG GIRL WHO SOUGHT THRILLS IN CRIME-- SHE SOON FOUND OUT THAT CRIME NEVER PAYS!

13

THE BOSS WAS RIGHT! POOR OLD POP DOESN'T KNOW WHICH END IS UP! WHAT A BLIND HE MAKES!

YEAH--YEAH-- THE BOSS SURE KNOWS HIS OATS, USING A SAP LIKE POP FOR A FALL GUY!

IN THE NEXT FEW DAYS, THERE WAS A FLOW OF NEW CUSTOMERS INTO POP'S STORE...

CIGARETTES, GIMME CIGARETTES!

CIGARETTES, HE SAYS. THERE ARE MANY BRANDS. NAME YOUR BRAND, MISTER.

DON'T KID ME. DON'T KID ME! I WANT THE SPECIAL KIND. THE SPECIAL KIND!

ALL RIGHT, ALL RIGHT. DON'T GET EXCITED. SUCH RUDENESS.

THREE DOLLARS FOR SIX CIGA-RETTES. I DON'T UNDERSTAND-- ALREADY THOSE CIGARETTES THOSE MEN GAVE ME ARE GONE. MISTER, WHAT'S IN THESE CIGARETTES, GOLD?

GOLD? ARE YOU KIDDING, POP?

SUCH STRANGE PEOPLE BUY MY CIGARETTES. STRANGE, STRANGE PEOPLE. AH, IT'S FOOLISHNESS, BUT WHEN THOSE FELLOWS COME BACK, I'LL MAKE A BIG RE-ORDER. I NEVER HAD SUCH A BIG DEMAND FOR CIGARETTES.

AND THAT NIGHT, IN A BACK ALLEY, THE STACCATO CRACK OF REVOLVER SHOTS SOUND OUT IN THE NIGHT, AS POLICEMEN CORNER A DESPERATE GUNMAN...

SURRENDER, YOU FOOL! HE MUST BE CRAZY, FIGHTING LIKE THIS. LET HIM HAVE IT, EDWARDS!

YOU BET, LIEUTEN-ANT!

CRACK! CRACK!

I'LL BLAST YOU! I'LL ...

OHHH!

MARIHUANA CIGARETTES! THAT EXPLAINS WHY HE SHOT IT OUT! SOME MARIHUANA RING HAS PROBABLY MOVED INTO TOWN...WE'LL HAVE TO CRACK THIS RING BEFORE IT SPREADS.

2

GOOD MORNING, POP. WHAT'S WRONG? YOU LOOK A LITTLE PALE. SOMETHING TROUBLING YOU?

AH, LIEUTENANT HENDERSON, WHAT A TERRIBLE THING THAT WAS LAST NIGHT. THE SHOOTING.

HMM, I'M OUT OF SMOKES. GUESS I'LL BUY A PACK!

THIS POOR FELLOW. THE ONE THAT WAS SHOT. HE WAS A CUSTOMER OF MINE. ONLY YESTERDAY I SOLD HIM A CIGARETTE.

IT'S QUEER. YOU BUY FOR TWENTY ONE CENTS, A WHOLE PACK OF CIGARETTES. HE PAID FIFTY CENTS FOR A CIGARETTE... A *SINGLE CIGARETTE!*

WHAT! WHAT'S THAT YOU'RE SAYING? FIFTY CENTS A CIGARETTE! WHAT KIND OF CIGARETTE!

A *SPECIAL KIND*. SOME SALESMEN GAVE ME SAMPLES. THEY SAID TO CHARGE *FIFTY CENTS APIECE*, AND I'D HAVE PLENTY OF CUSTOMERS. THEY WERE RIGHT. THE CIGARETTES ARE GONE ALREADY.

POP, LISTEN CAREFULLY. WOULD YOU KNOW ONE OF THESE *SPECIAL CIGARETTES* IF YOU SAW ONE AGAIN?

OF COURSE. ALL MY LIFE I'M IN THE TOBACCO BUSINESS. TOBACCO LIKE THIS.. *I NEVER SAW BEFORE,* VERY DARK TOBACCO. SURE, I'D KNOW IT.

WERE THEY LIKE *THESE?*

YEAH, YEAH, SURE. THESE ARE THE SPECIALS. TELL ME, LIEUTENANT, SOMEBODY ELSE IS SELLING THEM TOO?

THESE ARE SPECIAL CIGARETTES ALL RIGHT. DID YOU EVER HEAR OF A MARIHUANA, POP? HERE ARE THE CIGARETTES WE TOOK FROM THE DEAD BODY OF THAT DEAD GUNMAN. DO YOU KNOW WHAT YOU SOLD, POP?

NO, WHAT DID I DO? IS SOMETHING WRONG?

THESE CIGARETTES ARE POISON, POP. AS DEADLY AS BULLETS. VICIOUS, GREEDY RACKETEERS PEDDLE THEM TO WEAK PEOPLE, POP. MARIHUANA IS A DRUG, THAT WRECKS LIVES--AND CAUSES ONLY UNHAPPINESS.

3

I SOLD THOSE **THINGS?** I? **TAKE ME!** PUT ME IN PRISON! I'M A **FOOL!** I SHOULD HAVE KNOWN THAT NOTHING HONEST IS SO EXPENSIVE...

NO, POP. IT WASN'T YOUR FAULT. YOU'RE JUST THE FALL GUY. BUT YOU CAN HELP US.

WE'RE PROBABLY DEALING WITH A DRUG SYNDICATE. THEY PASS THE WORD AROUND TO KNOWN USERS OF MARIHUANA, THAT THEY'VE ESTABLISHED A NEW DISTRIBUTION POINT. SOMETIMES, THE DISTRIBUTOR IS INNOCENT, LIKE YOU--MORE OFTEN HE IS IN ON THE DEAL.

HERE'S WHAT I WANT YOU TO DO, POP. ACT AS IF NOTHING UNUSUAL HAS HAPPENED. WE'LL WATCH YOUR STORE DAY AND NIGHT, AND WHEN THOSE MEN COME BACK, WE'LL BE ABLE TO TRAIL THEM. THEY'RE PEANUTS. WE WANT TO GET THE HEAD OF THE RING. OKAY?

I'LL DO WHATEVER YOU SAY!

FOR THE NEXT FEW DAYS, A CEASELESS POLICE VIGIL WAS ESTABLISHED OVER POP'S STORE...

NOTHING DOING, DAN DO YOU THINK WE WASTED ALL THIS TIME? MAYBE THEY WERE SCARED OFF.

THESE BIRDS DON'T SCARE SO EASILY! THEY'LL BE BACK.

CIGARS
CIGAR
CIGARETTE

AND THEN...

WE'RE BACK, POP. HOW DID OUR SAMPLES GO?

ER--GOOD--THEY WENT FAST. THEY SOLD.

WHAT'S EATING YOU, POP?

WE DON'T MAKE YOU NERVOUS, DO WE, POP?

NO--UH-- **NO.** IT'S JUST--IT'S WARM--I FEEL WARM--

ACROSS THE STREET..

JOE, **LOOK!** POP'S WIPING HIS BROW! THAT'S THE SIGNAL! THOSE ARE THE MEN!

FRANK DID MAKE A MISTAKE, HE UNDER-ESTIMATED THE COURAGE OF A BRAVE OLD MAN...

SO LONG, COPPER! YEOW!

THEN, LIKE A TERRIER POUNCING ON A RAT...

NOW IT'S YOU AND ME, SMART GUY!

UFFF!

NOT SO TOUGH WITHOUT YOUR GUN, EH?

GET ME POLICE HEADQUARTERS.

OW!

A LITTLE LATER...

THAT WAS A BRAVE THING YOU DID, POP!

BRAVE? NOT BRAVE, DAN. I'M AN OLD MAN. ALL MY LIFE, I HAVE LIVED HONEST. THIS, I HAD TO DO, SUCH A LITTLE ACT, AGAINST SUCH A GREAT EVIL.

YOU'RE RIGHT, POP, NOW WE'LL HAVE TO GET THE REST OF THE MOB-- AND FIND OUT WHERE THEY'RE GROWING THE STUFF. THIS MUG WE CAUGHT WILL TALK. THEY ALWAYS DO.

AT POLICE HEADQUARTERS...

YOU DON'T HAVE A CHANCE, FRANK. HERE'S ALL THE EVIDENCE WE NEED. YOU'RE GOING TO TAKE THE RAP-- HARD. YOUR SIDE KICK IS DEAD. IF YOU DON'T TALK, THE BIG SHOT'LL BE RUNNING AROUND FREE, WHILE YOU'RE ROTTING IN JAIL.

I-I--ALL RIGHT-- I'LL TALK!

MASON, COME IN WITH YOUR BOOK. FRANK IS WILLING TO TALK.

6

GEE, BOSS--THIS IS A SWELL SPREAD, THIS REEFER RACKET. WE GROW THE STUFF OUT IN THESE LOTS, AN' THEN WE ROLL THE REEFERS RIGHT HERE. IT'S SOME DEAL.

AND WITH SMART OPERATORS LIKE FRANK AND CHARLIE, WE'LL ALWAYS FIND SAPS TO SELL IT--EITHER THEY'RE DUMB LIKE POP OR GREEDY FOR THE DOUGH. YES, PETE, BUT WHO CARES AS LONG AS GUYS LIKE US GET RICH.

YUH KNOW-- BOSS, I'D LIKE TO TRY ONE OF THEM CIGARETTES. WHAT'S WRONG, BOSS?

SHUT UP! MARIHUANA IS FOR SAPS AND SPINELESS JELLYFISH! IT MAKES YOU GOOFY-- WEAK UPSTAIRS! LET THE WEAK-LINGS SMOKE IT--WE DISH IT OUT--WE GET RICH ON IT, SEE?

NOBODY KNOWS WHAT A POISON IT IS LIKE WE DO. DON'T NEVER LET ME HEAR YOU TALK ABOUT SMOKING THEM AGAIN-- OR YOU'RE THROUGH! I NEED CLEAR THINKERS AROUND ME--NOT HOP HEADS!

YEAH, BOSS, I WAS ONLY KIDDING!

I WONDER WHAT'S DELAYING FRANK AND CHARLEY? WELL--THEY'LL BE HERE. THEY HAD A LOT OF CALLS TO MAKE.

SURE, BOSS-- THEY'LL BE BACK ANY TIME NOW!

AND IN A POLICE SQUAD CAR, RAPIDLY APPROACHING THE HEADQUARTERS OF THE MARIHUANA GANG...

THAT'S THE PLACE DOWN THE STREET, DRIVER. GET SET, BOYS, WE'RE MOVING IN FAST!

SWIFTLY, AND SILENTLY, THE POLICE EFFICIENTLY SURROUNDED THE RAMSHACKLE BUILDING--AND THE TRAP WAS CLOSED...

INSIDE...

COPS! THEY MUST'VE GRABBED FRANK AND CHARLEY! LET'S SCRAM, PETE!

DROP THAT GUN AND REACH!

THEY CAN'T STOP US, BOSS! LET'S EXIT OUT THE WINDOW!

I'LL GO FIRST!

BUT PETE DISCOVERED THAT THE ONLY EXIT FOR A GUNMAN IS···

AGH!

CRACK!

WHERE DO YOU THINK YOU'RE GOING, PAL? STAND WHERE YOU ARE OR I'LL DROP YOU!

D-D-DON'T SHOOT!

SOON:

LIEUTENANT, WE FOUND THE MARIHUANA PATCH. THEY WERE RAISING IT IN A COUPLE OF EMPTY LOTS.

GOOD. KEEP SOME OF IT FOR EVIDENCE, AND DESTROY THE REST···

8

MARIHUANA IS A THIEF THAT ROBS USERS OF STRENGTH, HEALTH AND SANITY. WHEN PEOPLE UNDERSTAND THAT NOTHING -- NOTHING CAN BE GAINED BUT MISERY FROM THE USE OF MARIHUANA·· THEY'LL STOP. THEN THIS EVIL WILL BE ERASED FROM OUR SOCIETY.

DON'T WORRY, THE COPS JUST WANT HIM FOR QUESTIONING! THEY'RE ASKING ALL THE **"EAGLE"** BOYS ABOUT A MUGGING UPTOWN!

LET'S GET OUT OF HERE, JIMMY! TAKE ME SOMEPLACE WHERE THE AIR IS COOL AND CLEANER...

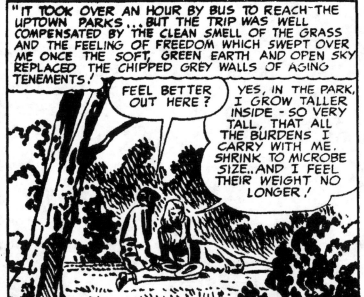

"IT TOOK OVER AN HOUR BY BUS TO REACH THE UPTOWN PARKS...BUT THE TRIP WAS WELL COMPENSATED BY THE CLEAN SMELL OF THE GRASS AND THE FEELING OF FREEDOM WHICH SWEPT OVER ME ONCE THE SOFT, GREEN EARTH AND OPEN SKY REPLACED THE CHIPPED GREY WALLS OF AGING TENEMENTS!"

FEEL BETTER OUT HERE?

YES, IN THE PARK, I GROW TALLER INSIDE - SO VERY TALL, THAT ALL THE BURDENS I CARRY WITH ME, SHRINK TO MICROBE SIZE..AND I FEEL THEIR WEIGHT NO LONGER!

FUNNY, THERE SEEMS TO BE ENOUGH LAND AND SKY FOR **EVERY** MAN! YET WE'RE JAMMED TOGETHER BY THE THOUSANDS ON ONE GARBAGE HEAP SO THAT NONE OF US CAN SEE THE SUN!

NOR EVER BE TRULY CONTENT!

WE'LL **BEAT** THIS SETUP, YOU AND I! JUST WAIT AND SEE, MEG! SOMEDAY SOON, WE'LL BREAK OUT OF THAT BRICK PRISON AND MAKE FOR THE OPEN SPACES... BUY A **FARM** OR SOMETHING!

OH, JIMMY... LET'S GO RIGHT AWAY... BEFORE IT'S TOO LATE! BEFORE THE STREET DEVOURS US...AND WE BECOME PART OF IT!

YES, MEG! IT WON'T BE LONG... I PROMISE YOU!

JIMMY - JIMMY!

"THE ABRUPT CONTRAST UPON RETURNING TO THE STREET WAS LIKE A HARSH GRATING ON THE SENSES! THE MORBID, GLOOM WAS MORE APPARENT THAN EVER! POP'S ROARING VOICE WHEN I ENTERED THE FLAT, WAS A FINAL TOUCH THAT MADE THE DEPRESSING PICTURE COMPLETE!"

POP! WHAT'S WRONG?

TAKE A **LOOK!** LOOK WHO'S BACK!

AW! STOW IT. I AIN'T STAYIN'!

2

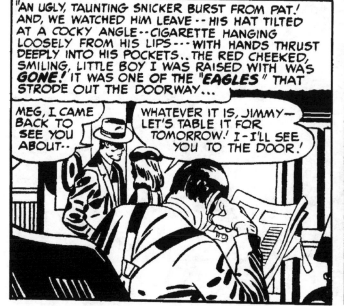

3

AND, I TELL YOU THAT **NOTHING'S** GOING TO HAPPEN! WE'LL WORK! SAVE!--AND, FINALLY GET OUT OF THIS RAT HOLE! ALL OF US! YOU'VE GOT TO BELIEVE THAT, MEG!

I-I BELIEVE YOU, JIMMY! IT WILL BE JUST AS YOU SAY!

"IT WAS THAT HOPE THAT KEPT MY SPIRIT ALIVE IN THE MONTHS THAT FOLLOWED! I WAS WORKING AS A SALESGIRL IN ONE OF THE LARGER DEPARTMENT STORES! AND JIMMY WAS EMPLOYED AS A CLERK IN A MAIL-ORDER HOUSE... THE EAGERNESS TO ADVANCE OUR POSITIONS RESULTED IN SMALL RAISES FROM TIME TO TIME..OUR BATTLE AGAINST THE STREET SEEMED TO BE TURNING IN OUR FAVOR!

TELEPHONE CALL FOR YOU, MEG! I CAN WAIT ON THE LADY!

THANKS, MARY! WOULD YOU EXCUSE ME FOR A MOMENT, MADAM--

OF COURSE, MY DEAR!

JIMMY! I'M SO GLAD YOU CALLED! MISTER GIDDENS CALLED ME INTO HIS OFFICE THIS MORNING AND--**JIMMY**--ARE YOU LISTENING?

MEG--I JUST QUIT MY JOB! I WAS SLATED FOR A BETTER POSITION IN THE UPTOWN BRANCH! BUT THEY PASSED ME UP-- "**WRONG BACKGROUND!**" I BLEW MY TOP AND TOOK OFF!

OH, **NO!** BUT, JIMMY! IT WASN'T NECESSARY TO **QUIT!** YOU COULD HAVE STAYED ON UNTIL YOU FOUND ANOTHER OPPORTUNITY ELSEWHERE!

AW, WHAT'S THE USE! SEE YOU LATER BABY--I'M HANGING UP!

"I ALMOST SWORE AT THE IMPOTENCE OF THE TELEPHONE! THE DISTANCE BETWEEN US MADE IT IMPOSSIBLE FOR ME TO REASON WITH HIM... THE CYNICISM AND BITTERNESS OF THE STREET WAS IN HIS VOICE WHEN JIMMY HUNG UP ON ME...

I'VE GOT TO KEEP HIM FROM BECOMING DISCOURAGED-- OR EVERYTHING WE'RE STRIVING FOR IS **LOST!**

4

"IT TOOK ME AN HOUR TO LOCATE JIMMY AFTER I EMERGED FROM THE SUBWAY!.. I FOUND HIM ON A STREET CORNER IN CASUAL CONVERSATION WITH TWO BOYS HE CALLED *ROXY* AND *PORK-CHOPS!* THE WORD *"HAWKS"* EMBLAZONED ON THEIR LOUD JACKETS TOLD THE REST OF THEIR STORY!

S'CUSE ME, FELLAS! HI, MEG!

JIMMY-- MAY I TALK TO YOU?

SAY AIN'T SHE PAT'S SISTER, MEG? NICE CHICK, JIMMY! WHY DON'T YOU BRING HER DOWN TO THE CLUB SOME NIGHT.. WELL-- SEE YOU AROUND!

YEAH-- OKAY, ROXY! SO LONG, PORK CHOPS!

YOU KNOW ROXY AND PORK CHOPS, DON'T YOU?

DO I *HAVE* TO?

AND DO *YOU?* THERE'S BETTER COMPANY TO MIX WITH ON THE STREET THAN THOSE TWO! ROXY AND PORK CHOPS BELONG TO A CROWD THAT'S PRETTY BAD MEDICINE, JIMMY!

AW-- THEY'RE NO WORSE THAN ANYONE ELSE ON THE BLOCK! BESIDES, I HAD TO TALK TO *SOME-BODY* TO KEEP MY MIND OFF WHAT HAPPENED AT THE OFFICE TODAY!

OH, I KNOW HOW BITTER YOU MUST FEEL ABOUT THAT, JIMMY... BUT IT'S ONLY A *TEMPORARY* SETBACK-- NOT A COMPLETE COLLAPSE OF HOPE!

HUH! I'VE GOT A *POOR BACK-GROUND*, THEY SAID! IS THAT MY FAULT? DID I *ASK* TO BE BORN IN THIS ROTTEN NEIGHBOR-HOOD?

YOU'LL GET ANOTHER JOB, JIMMY! YOU'RE INTELLIGENT! YOU'VE GOT ABILITY! THERE'S NO REASON WHY YOU CAN'T MAKE GOOD!

SURE! I *GET* ANOTHER JOB! -- GIVE IT ALL I'VE GOT-- I'M THE FAIR-HAIRED BOY-- THEN *BOOM!*

5

IT'S GOING TO HAPPEN AGAIN AND AGAIN, BABY! BRAINS DON'T COUNT! IF YOU'RE BORN ON THE STREET -- YOU **STAY** ON THE STREET!

NOW, WHO'S CRYING--?

I AIN'T CRYING! I'M SORE! UNDERSTAND? **SORE!** I **WORKED** FOR THAT PROMOTION! REALLY EARNED IT! AND **WHAT** DID I GET IN RETURN? WHY SHOULDN'T I BLOW OFF STEAM?

BUT YOU DON'T HAVE TO TAKE IT OUT ON THE **WHOLE WORLD,** JIMMY! PERHAPS **ANOTHER** FIRM WILL APPRECIATE YOU?

YEAH! I'LL BE PRESIDENT OF THE COMPANY IN NO TIME AT ALL! JIMMY ROSE-- **BOY TYCOON!**

DON'T DO THAT, JIMMY! --YOU-YOU **SCARE** ME--

YOU SOUND LIKE ONE OF **THEM** -- LIKE ROXY OR PORK CHOPS! IT ISN'T LIKE YOU, JIMMY. AND I'M SCARED! IF YOU KEEP ON ACTING LIKE THIS-- WE'LL **NEVER** BREAK AWAY FROM THE STREET!

AW, MEG-- I'D RATHER CUT MY ARM OFF THAN MAKE YOU FEEL DOWN IN THE DUMPS! C'MON, I'LL BUY YOU A SODA BEFORE I WALK YOU HOME!

ALL RIGHT, JIMMY! BUT YOU'VE GOT TO PROMISE ME THAT YOU'LL TRY FOR ANOTHER JOB-- AND MAKE GOOD-- FOR **US!**

"JIMMY PROMISED... BUT HIS TONE WAS COLD AND VAGUE.. I SAW VERY LITTLE OF HIM IN THE WEEKS THAT FOLLOWED.. IN THE FEW TIMES WE MANAGED TO DATE, I COULDN'T HELP BUT NOTICE THE CHANGES IN JIMMY'S MANNER--CHANGES THAT WERE NEITHER SUBTLE NOR BENEFICIAL! **THE MARK OF THE STREET WAS FORMING ON JIMMY--** I WAS SICK WITH WORRY...

WHERE'S **PAT** TONIGHT?

HOW SHOULD I KNOW? HE NEVER TELLS ME WHERE HE GOES!

6

I SEE **YOU'RE** NOT STAYIN' HOME EITHER, MISS HIGH AND MIGHTY! WHERE ARE YOU GOING **NOW?**

I'VE ALREADY HAD SUPPER.. I'M GOING TO LOOK FOR JIMMY ROSE!

HUH! **THAT** YOUNG DRIFTER WON'T BE HARD TO FIND! I SAW HIM IN MIKE'S POOLROOM WHEN I PASSED ON MY WAY HOME! WHAT'S THE MATTER? DON'T HE BELIEVE IN **WORKING** ANY MORE?

I—I'LL SEE YOU LATER, POP!

"THERE WAS ONLY ONE WORD FOR MIKE'S POOL ROOM! -- **UNCLEAN!** THE SMOKE-FILLED AIR, THE MALCONTENTS WHO BREATHED IT AND THE OBSCENE LANGUAGE ERUPTING HARSHLY IN THE COILING MURK WERE THE VISUAL EXPRESSIONS OF THE WORD... WHAT HURT ME MOST WAS FINDING JIMMY THERE -- AND REALIZING THAT **HE DIDN'T LOOK OUT OF PLACE!!**

JIMMY—

SH-H-H!

WHY— MEG! I DIDN'T EXPECT TO SEE **YOU** HERE!

THAT'S **MY** LINE, JIMMY! DO YOU THINK YOU CAN TEAR YOURSELF AWAY FROM THAT GAME? I'D LIKE TO TALK TO YOU!

HOW DO YOU LIKE THE **NERVE** OF THAT CHICK! AIN'TCHA LEARNED HOW TO TRAIN A BROAD YET, JIMMY?

DROP THAT CRUMMY OLD **POOL STICK**, JIMMEE! BABY WANTS TO CHEW THE RAG!

HA-HA-HA--

"JIMMY'S COMPANIONS WERE MOCKING AND OFFENSIVE... BUT INSTEAD OF BEING AROUSED, BY THEIR BEHAVIOR, JIMMY SCOWLED DARKLY AT ME AND HURRIED ME OUT INTO THE STREET! THE RESOUNDING ECHOES OF LAUGHTER FOLLOWED US THROUGH THE DOOR...

FOR PETE'S SAKE, MEG! WHAT ARE YOU TRYING TO DO? MAKE ME LOOK LIKE A JERK?

JIMMY, YOU'RE **HURTING** ME!

7

8

"MY PLEADING MADE NO IMPRESSION ON JIMMY! I BEGAN TO CRY! SOMETHING IN HIS EYES STIRRED WITH PAIN... AND HE MADE AS IF TO SPEAK! BUT IT WAS THE VOICES OF **SLINK** AND HIS FRIENDS I HEARD--SNEERING AND IMPATIENT! **JIMMY JOINED THEM**.. I WAS STILL CRYING WHEN THEY WERE SMALL SILHOUETTES IN THE DISTANCE...

"DESPITE HIS SURRENDER TO **THE STREET**, I COULDN'T STOP LOVING JIMMY! OUR DESCENT LED TO THE **HAWK'S** CELLAR CLUB — A LARGE, SHABBY ROOM IN THE BASEMENT OF AN OLD BROWNSTONE BUILDING... IT WAS THERE THAT I WOULD WAIT LONG, FEARFUL HOURS FOR JIMMY TO SHOW UP-- **AFRAID** OF WHAT HE MIGHT BE DOING...

WANNA DANCE WHILE YOU WAIT FOR JIMMY?

NO, I DON'T, JINGLES!

WHATSAMATTER? AM I **UGLY** OR SOMETHIN'?

DON'T BUILD UP A CASE! I JUST **DON'T** WANT TO DANCE, THAT'S ALL!

WHY FOOL WITH A MOPE LIKE **HER**, JINGLES? I THINK YOU'RE A LIVING DOLL! C'MON! LET'S PLAY A BOP RECORD!

AND WHO ASKED **YOU** TO BUTT IN WITH YOUR TWO CENTS, ANGIE--.

NOW, GO ON! BEAT IT! I DON'T WANTCHA TO BOTHER ME WHEN I'M **BUSY**!

LOOK, BABE! WHEN JINGLES ASKS A DAME TO DANCE WITH HIM SHE **DANCES**, SEE?

LET ME GO, YOU BUM! I'M NOT YOUR PROPERTY!

10

"A LITTLE LATER, THE POLICE WALKED IN—TWO NEIGHBORHOOD COPS NAMED GALLAGHER AND ROSS AND A PLAINCLOTHESMAN... THEY BEGAN ASKING QUESTIONS--THEIR COLD, PIERCING EYES PROBING EACH MASK OF FEIGNED INNOCENCE...

WHAT'S UP, OFFICER? ANYTHING WRONG?

I KNOW YOU TWO KIDS. I'M KINDA SORRY TO SEE YOU HERE! YOU'VE BOTH BEEN CLEAN UP TO NOW!

WHAT DO YOU MEAN UP TO NOW? WE'RE JUST HAVING A NICE LITTLE PARTY, THAT'S ALL!

IT'S NO USE TALKING TO YOU! BUT YOUR GIRL FRIEND STILL LOOKS ON THE LEVEL... WHICH OF THESE BOYS WERE HERE ALL DAY--AND WHICH OF THEM JUST CAME IN, HONEY?

EVERY ONE OF US HAS BEEN HERE SINCE EIGHT! JIMMY ISN'T LYING -- WE'VE BEEN HAVING A PARTY!

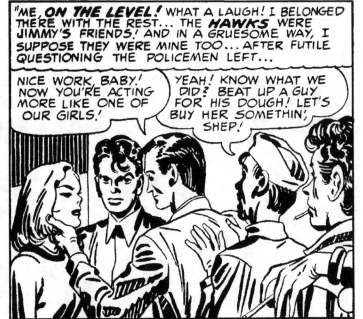

"ME, ON THE LEVEL! WHAT A LAUGH! I BELONGED THERE WITH THE REST... THE HAWKS WERE JIMMY'S FRIENDS! AND IN A GRUESOME WAY, I SUPPOSE THEY WERE MINE TOO... AFTER FUTILE QUESTIONING THE POLICEMEN LEFT...

NICE WORK, BABY! NOW YOU'RE ACTING MORE LIKE ONE OF OUR GIRLS!

YEAH! KNOW WHAT WE DID? BEAT UP A GUY FOR HIS DOUGH! LET'S BUY HER SOMETHIN', SHEP!

MAYBE WE WILL, MEG! GOT A GOOD HAUL! A HUNDRED BUCKS! SAY, HOW ABOUT A DANCE? IT'LL HELP YOU GET OVER THAT SHYNESS!

"OVER SHEP'S SHOULDER, I COULD SEE JIMMY'S FACE! IT WAS DARK AND TENSE! BUT HE DIDN'T INTERFERE... HE HAD EMBRACED THE CODE OF THE HAWKS... AND, NOW, IT WAS STRANGLING HIM! I FELT SORRY FOR HIM! SORRY FOR US! I GLIDED ALONG WITH SHEP.. HE WAS A SMOOTH DANCER...

12

"MAYBE IT'S THE WAY YOU FEEL INSIDE THAT AFFECTS YOUR APPEARANCE, BUT, IN THE DAYS THAT FOLLOWED, I DIDN'T RECOGNIZE THE GIRL WHO FACED ME FROM MY MIRROR... SHE WAS A TYPICAL MEMBER OF THE *HAWKS!* CYNICAL! BRASSY! NOT THE KIND OF GIRL WHO COULD KEEP THE JOB I HAD... THAT'S WHY I LOST IT!

THAT'S THE SECOND TIME THIS WEEK A CUSTOMER HAS REPORTED YOU FOR DISCOURTESY, MISS O'BRIEN. WHAT HAVE YOU TO SAY THIS TIME?

I JUST COULDN'T PLEASE THE OLD HAG! SHE GOT ON MY NERVES!

THEN, IF THAT'S YOUR ATTITUDE, I'M AFRAID I SHALL HAVE TO *DISCHARGE* YOU! THIS STORE CAN'T AFFORD TO EMPLOY SALESGIRLS WHO CAN'T BE PATIENT WITH ITS CUSTOMERS!

WHY DON'T YOU STOP FLAPPIN' YOUR JAW! IT'S ENOUGH I'M CANNED! I DON'T NEED ANY OF YOUR ROTTEN LECTURES!

"MY INSOLENCE WAS ONLY A SHALLOW FRONT TO HIDE MY FEAR AND DETECTION... I DIDN'T LIKE LOSING MY JOB... IT MEANT TROUBLE AT HOME – AND A PERIOD OF IDLENESS IN WHICH MY MIND COULD DWELL ON THE PURPOSELESS EXISTENSE I WAS LEADING... POP WAS MAD AS A HORNET WHEN HE HEARD ABOUT IT!

NO WONDER YOU LOST YOUR JOB! YOU'RE GETTIN' TO BE LIKE THOSE BUMS YOU GO OUT WITH!

OH! LEAVE ME ALONE!

DON'T *YOU* BE GIVING ME THAT KIND OF TALK! I NEVER TOOK THE STRAP TO YOU YET! BUT I CAN *START* ANY TIME YOU GET ME MAD ENOUGH!

ALL I'VE HEARD IS BELLY ACHING TODAY! I'M GOING DOWN TO THE *HAWKS'* CLUB AND RELAX! SEE YOU LATER!

GO AHEAD! GO AHEAD! THERE'S NO HOPE HERE ON THE STREET! NOT EVEN IN THE CHILDREN! NO HOPE! NO PRIDE! IT'S A SORRY LOT WE ARE!

"*NO HOPE! NO PRIDE!* POP'S WORDS BIT DEEPLY LIKE THE PAINFUL THRUST OF A BLADE IN THE FLESH! HIS LABORIOUS EXISTENCE HAD DRAINED THE TENDERNESS FROM HIM! BUT HE WAS A HUMAN BEING AND COULD FEEL DESPAIR! *I HATED MYSELF! I HATED THE GARBAGE SMELL OF MY SOUL! IT WOULD TAKE MORE THAN TEARS TO WASH IT CLEAN...*

HEY! THERE'S *MEG!* LOOKS LIKE SHE'S GOT THE BLUES AGAIN!

DEAL ME OUT OF THIS HAND... I WANNA TALK TO HER!

13

I WON'T BE GOOD COMPANY TONIGHT, SHEP! IF IT'S ALL THE SAME TO YOU, I'D JUST LIKE TO MOPE AROUND BY MYSELF!

I KNOW WHAT'S EATIN' YOU, KID.. HEARD YOU LOST YOUR JOB! TOO BAD! BUT I'VE GOT A DEAL YOU MIGHT GO FOR.. EASY WORK.. SHORT HOURS..

THERE'S NOTHING TO IT! AND THE SPLIT IS GOOD! ALL YOU DO IS GIVE A CHUMP THE GLAD EYE.. LET HIM PICK YOU UP! THEN LEAD HIM TO WHERE ME AND THE BOYS ARE WAITIN'! WE DO THE REST! HOW ABOUT IT?

SHE AIN'T GONNA DO NOTHING OF THE SORT, SHEP! GET AWAY FROM HER!

STILL THE FRESH, LOUD-MOUTHED PUNK, AIN'TCHA, JIMMY! I'LL GIVE YOU A SECOND TO TAKE YOUR HANDS OFF MY SHIRT!

YEAH! I'M A BUM! THAT'S WHAT I'VE BECOME, SHEP! BUT I'LL BE HANGED IF I'LL LET YOU TALK MEG INTO BEING ONE!

"JIMMY AND SHEP ALMOST STRUCK SIMULTANEOUSLY! THE VIOLENCE THAT BURST FROM THEM WAS THE FRIGHTFUL TOOTH-AND-CLAW FURY OF MADDENED ANIMALS! THE STREET, LIKE THE JUNGLE, KNEW NO RULES FOR COMBAT!

"SHEP FOUGHT WITH THE ANGER OF INJURED ARROGANCE! BUT JIMMY WAS PURGING HIM-SELF OF THE FILTH WHICH WAS BLACKENING THE WALLS OF HIS HEART!! EVERY TERRIBLE THING INSIDE JIMMY LEAPED INTO OPEN SIGHT AND STRIPPED HIM OF ALL HUMANITY!!

14

"THE GANG CLUSTERED AT THE EDGE OF THE CONFLICT--HELD IN CHECK BY THE INCREDIBLE FEROCITY WHICH LASHED OUT IN ALL DIRECTIONS--FORCING BACK ALL THOSE IT THREATENED TO TOUCH!

HEY! THAT JIMMY'S REALLY *RUINING* SHEP! LET'S RUSH HIM!

YOU RUSH HIM! I JUST GOT A NEW SUIT!

JIMMY! JIMMY! YOU'RE HURT!

I COULDN'T STAND IT ANY LONGER, MEG! I GAVE *MYSELF* UP FOR LOST! BUT I COULDN'T STAND WHAT WAS HAPPENING TO *YOU!* MEG-- MEG--

I LOVE YOU, JIMMY! IT WAS *BECAUSE* I LOVE YOU THAT I FOLLOWED YOU INTO ALL THIS!

MEG AND I ARE GETTIN' OUT OF HERE! IF ANYBODY HAS ANY IDEAS ABOUT JUMPIN' ME-- FORGET IT! I'M MAD ENOUGH TO PLAY *FOR KEEPS!*

"JIMMY AND I ASCENDED FROM THE BASEMENT INTO THE MOONLIT STREET-- HAND IN HAND-- KNOWING EACH OTHER AS WE NEVER DID BEFORE...

"AROUND US ON EVERY SIDE TOWERED THE DARKENED TENEMENTS -- BROODING SYMBOLS OF *THE STREET* -- THE STREET WHICH WAS POWERLESS IN THE FACE OF THE UNDAUNTED SPIRIT! JIMMY GRIPPED MY HAND TIGHTLY.. WE WOULD TRY AGAIN.. I FELT THE EXHILARATING SURGE OF *HOPE!*

SHE DEFIED AUTHORITY, THIS HARDENED PRODUCT OF THE CELLAR CLUBS, BUT SHE COULD NOT DEFY THE LOVE THAT LED HER ASTRAY, AND TURNED HER INTO A...

REFORM SCHOOL GIRL!

AT THE GIRLS' REFORMATORY FOR SEVEN MONTHS... HATING IT... AND NOW HATING THESE SMUG MEN AND WOMEN OF THE PAROLE BOARD...

YOU WANT TO KNOW WHY I THINK I'M READY FOR PAROLE, EH? WELL--I WAS HERE ON A BUM RAP IN THE FIRST PLACE.

I COULD HEAR THE QUICK INTAKE OF BREATH ON THE PART OF SOME OF THE BOARD MEMBERS. I WENT ON!"MAYBE YOU'RE TOO OLD TO KNOW WHAT IT'S LIKE TO GO FOR A GUY LIKE JEFF NASON.".

COULD YOU GO FOR ME, JEFF, IF I MADE MYSELF LOOK LIKE YOU WANT ME TO?

WHY NOT? YOU COULD BE A SLICK CHICK, IF YOU TRIED.

"I WAS STILL FLOATING ON AIR THE NEXT AFTER-NOON. IF IT MEANT ONLY DRESSING DIFFERENTLY TO MAKE JEFF GO FOR ME!.."

THE BIG STORE! THEY REALLY HAVE BARGAINS...

"I KNEW PA'D GRIPE ABOUT HOLDING OUT ON MY PAY FROM THE FACTORY. LET HIM. I DIDN'T OWE THEM A THING AT HOME. THEY COULD ONLY NAG SOME MORE."

QUIT SHOVIN'! I WAS JUST REACHING FOR THAT DRESS!

SHUT UP OR I'LL SHOVE IT DOWN YOUR THROAT!

"IF YOU WERE EVER AT A BASEMENT SALE, YOU'LL UNDERSTAND HOW I GOT THE IDEA IN A DRESSING ROOM..."

I'M NUTS TO PAY FOR THIS RAG! IN THIS MOB, I CAN WALK OUT WITH IT UNDER MY OWN DRESS!

"THE DRESS DID THINGS FOR ME. THAT NIGHT AT THE PUSHERS CLUB, JEFF REALLY GAVE ME A TUMBLE..."

LIKE IT, JEFF?

BABY, I'D NEVER KNOWN YOU! UMMMM!

"JEFF TOOK ME IN HIS ARMS AND KISSED ME AGAIN AND AGAIN LONG KISSES...OR, MAYBE YOU DON'T UNDERSTAND!..THERE WAS A SHOCKED SILENCE AMONG MEMBERS OF THE BOARD...

I CONTINUED "I SAW WHAT A CINCH IT WAS TO STEAL THE DRESS. WHY WOULDN'T IT WORK WITH OTHER THINGS? AND DON'T THINK IT DIDN'T!.."

JEFF'LL LOVE THESE! THE BROOCH AND EARRINGS!

"BUT JUST AS I WALKED OUT OF THE STORE..."

ALL RIGHT, MISS. YOU AND I ARE TAKING A WALK TO THE MANAGER'S OFFICE!

WHAT'S THE IDEA?

THAT'S ALL. IF IT'S A CRIME TO LOVE A GUY LIKE JEFF, AND BE BORN IN POVERTY, THEN... I'M GUILTY...

ONE MOMENT, YOUNG WOMAN!

WE SYMPATHIZE WITH YOU, BUT YOU ARE ASKING US TO JUSTIFY YOUR CRIMES!

THOUSANDS OF YOUNG PEOPLE HAVE SOLVED EVEN WORSE PROBLEMS!

I MIGHT HAVE KNOWN!

ONCE OUTSIDE, I VOWED...

IF THEY THINK I'M WAITING ANOTHER SIX MONTHS FOR A CHANCE TO GET OUT OF THIS PEN, THEY'RE CRAZY!

THE REFORMATORY WORKED ON AN HONOR SYSTEM. IT WAS A NATURAL FOR ME. ONE NIGHT A WEEK LATER, I WALKED INTO THE PUSHERS CLUB...

I'M BACK, JEFF!

FAITH BUTLER— MY BABY!

BABY! BABY!

JEFF! I'VE BEEN SO LONELY FOR YOU!

HOW DID YOU GET OUT SO SOON, BABY?

I JUST WALKED AWAY, JEFF! I HAD TO SEE YOU!

4

5

6

FIVE HUNDRED EVEN.

I'M GOING TO TOP THAT!

IT WAS A WEEK BEFORE I TOPPED FOUR NINETY, BUT I KEPT AT IT...

COME ON, FAITH... REST PERIOD. TAKE IT EASY.

NO, YOU GET A RHYTHM WHEN YOU KEEP AT IT. I'M STICKING HERE.

NO SMOKING

YOU DID IT, FAITH! FIVE HUNDRED AND TWELVE! YOU KNOW, I THINK YOU OUGHT TO MEET YOUR COMPETITOR. HE COMES ON AT FIVE...

I'D LIKE TO. HE OUGHT TO SEE THE WRECK HE'S MADE OF ME.

IT WAS THE END OF THE NEXT DAY THAT THE SUPERVISOR CALLED. I WAS JUST GETTING READY TO LEAVE...

HERE HE IS, FAITH. HE WANTED TO MEET THE GAL WHO BROKE HIS REC--- HEY, DO YOU TWO KNOW EACH OTHER?

JEFF!

FAITH!

JEFF WAS OLDER AND LOOKED IT AND THERE WAS SOMETHING DIFFERENT ABOUT HIM...

I'M GLAD IT'S YOU WHO BEAT MY RECORD, FAITH. I GUESS WE BOTH HAVE GROWN UP A LOT... IN THREE YEARS.

YOU... YOU LOOK WELL, JEFF. YOU... YOU'VE CHANGED TOO!

A LOT FOR THE BETTER, I HOPE. IT WAS HARD GROWING UP... THE WAY WE DID IT. BUT... I GUESS I'D CALL MYSELF A MAN NOW... THEY'VE OVERLOOKED MY PRISON RECORD. THEY'VE ACCEPTED ME IN THE AIR FORCE!

OH, NO, JEFF! SUPPOSE YOU..... GET HURT!

THAT DID IT. IN AN INSTANT, WE WERE IN EACH OTHER'S ARMS. YES, THINGS HAD CHANGED, BUT OUR LOVE HAD NOT. IT WAS JUST SANER NOW, AND MORE ENDURING. . .

FAITH.... FAITH...!

MY DARLING!

7

2

THAT NIGHT...

MAKE IT A STRIKE THIS TIME, KATHY! WE'RE WAY AHEAD!

JACK AND DOTTY ACT AS IF THEY'RE DRUNK! IT'S GETTING EMBARRASSING!

LATER...

WE BEAT YOU THREE GAMES STRAIGHT! BROTHER, FOR A FOUR-LETTER MAN ARE YOU SLIPPING!

SO WHAT?

HERE DOTTY ...LIGHT UP!

I'M NEXT AFTER BILL ...UNLESS KATHY WANTS TO TRY ONE!

NO THANKS, DOTTY... I TRIED A CIGARETTE ONCE, AND IT MADE MY HEAD SWIM!

GO AHEAD, HONEY... I TRIED ONE TODAY!

IS THAT MARIJUANA? BILL! I'M SURPRISED AT YOU!

I DON'T WANT ANYTHING TO DO WITH THIS! LET ME OUT RIGHT HERE!

AWWW...STOP ACTING LIKE A DRIP!

BUT...

SINCE WHEN DID SHE GET SO HIGH AND MIGHTY? WE'RE NOT GOOD ENOUGH FOR HER, HUH?

LET HER GO... SHE DON'T KNOW WHAT SHE'S MISSING...SEE YA TOMORROW, BILL!

3

IF YOU DIDN'T WANT ONE, O.K. ...BUT YOU DIDN'T HAVE TO TAKE A RUN-OUT POWDER AND SPOIL EVERYBODY ELSE'S FUN!

I'M NOT GETTING MIXED UP WITH THAT STUFF! IT'S A DRUG! IT'S DANGEROUS!

I'VE HAD TWO TODAY...DO I LOOK LIKE A DEAD MAN OR SOMETHING?

BILL! YOU'RE BEING FOOLISH!

...I CAN QUIT ANYTIME I WANT TO!

THREE MONTHS LATER... BILL STILL THINKS HE CAN QUIT ANY TIME BUT NOW HE DOESN'T WANT TO!

I CAN'T CONCENTRATE ON THIS STUFF ANY MORE ...GOTTA GET A COUPLE OF DRAGS FAST OR I'LL BLOW MY TOP!

BILL, I'D LIKE TO SEE YOU FOR A FEW MINUTES!

YES, SIR...

WE'VE ALWAYS BEEN FRIENDS, BILL ... YOUR WORK HASN'T BEEN UP TO PAR LATELY... WHAT'S WRONG?

I'M OKAY... JUST SORT OF LOSING INTEREST, I GUESS!

4

PERHAPS THAT AFTER-SCHOOL JOB INTERFERES WITH YOUR STUDIES...OR ARE YOU HAVING TROUBLE AT HOME?

I'M OKAY, I TOLD YOU! THERE'S NOTHING WRONG AT HOME OR ON THE JOB!

MEANWHILE...

HERE'S SIX BUCKS FOR 24 STICKS, CHARLEY...AND I GET SIX STICKS FOR COMMISSION — RIGHT?

NOT SO LOUD...

LOOKS LIKE YOU PICKED UP A COUPLE OF NEW CUSTOMERS!

YEAH... ONE NEW ONE...

KEEP IT UP...IF YOU SELL ENOUGH YOU GET YOUR OWN REEFERS FOR FREE!

DESPITE BILL'S PROTESTS, EVERY-THING WAS NOT ALL RIGHT IN THE STORE WHERE HE WORKED AFTER SCHOOL...

THAT'S THE FIFTH KICK WE'VE HAD ABOUT YOU TODAY, YOUNG MAN! I'M TIRED OF COMPLAINTS FROM CUSTOMERS! YOU'RE FIRED!

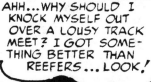

WHERE'LL I GET MONEY FOR STICKS NOW? I BETTER FIND JACK, QUICK!

OUT

FIRST I GET GRILLED BY OLD SEMPLE IN MATH-- THEN I GET FIRED FROM MY JOB!

RELAX, BOY! I GOT BOUNCED OFF THE TRACK TEAM TODAY...HOW D'YA LIKE THAT? LET'S FIND A BOOTH IN HERE AND SNEAK A BANG!

....GOSH! ONLY A COUPLE OF MONTHS AGO THE COACH WAS POINTING YOU FOR THE NATIONAL INTERSCHOLASTICS, TOO!

AHH...WHY SHOULD I KNOCK MYSELF OUT OVER A LOUSY TRACK MEET? I GOT SOME-THING BETTER THAN REEFERS...LOOK!

5

6

10

NEXT DAY...

GUESS WE'RE IN THE CLEAR ON THE ACCIDENT! HAVE YOU HEARD FROM JACK?

YEAH—HE CALLED ME UP LONG DISTANCE BUT WOULDN'T SAY WHERE HE WAS... SAID HE WAS GOING TO HIDE OUT!..

DOTTY, DID HE EVER TELL YOU WHERE HE GOT THE STUFF? I'M GOING CRAZY WITHOUT IT!

NO—BUT HE USED TO HANG AROUND CHARLEY'S STORE! LET'S TRY IT!

OH, GOD, I KNEW IT!.. WHEN I GO TOO LONG WITHOUT A SHOT, MY STOMACH TIES UP IN KNOTS!.. I... I CAN'T... STAND... IT...

IT'S GOT ME TOO!...COME ON!

HE'D BETTER SELL IT TO US IF HE'S GOT IT! I'M ABOUT READY TO BLOW UP!

WE'RE FRIENDS OF JACK'S! WE GOTTA HAVE A SHOT...QUICK!

BEAT IT KID... YA GOT THE WRONG PLACE!

DON'T LIE TO ME!.. I'LL... I'LL KILL YOU!

HEY—TAKE IT EASY! THE COPS MIGHTA FOLLOWED YOU HERE!

11

AT THE HOSPITAL...

WE'LL TREAT YOU HERE FOR THREE WEEKS — AFTER THAT YOU'LL BE AT HOME. IF YOU KEEP AWAY FROM DRUGS FOR SIX MONTHS, YOU CAN PROBABLY GET RID OF THIS ADDICTION.

OH, BILL, I KNOW YOU CAN DO IT!

SIX MONTHS WITHOUT THE STUFF, I'LL GO NUTS!

TWO NIGHTS LATER!

I'LL DO ANYTHING FOR A BANG... ANYTHING!

CHARLEY, I GOTTA HAVE IT... I'LL PAY YOU TOMORROW!

NOTHING DOING... BEAT IT PUNK!

JACK! AM I GLAD TO SEE YOU! TELL HIM HE'S GOT TO GIVE ME THE STUFF-- I'LL PAY HIM TOMORROW!

SURE HE'LL GIVE US "CAPS"-- WON'T YOU CHARLEY?

WELL, ALL RIGHT, BUT I WANT TO SEE THE MONEY TOMORROW! NOW BEAT IT!

HOLD IT BOYS!.. WE'RE TAKING YOU IN!

15

WATCH IT, ED... THIS KID'S GOT A GUN!

HE WON'T MAKE ANY TROUBLE!

WHY'D YOU HAVE TO PULL THAT GUN? THEY'LL THROW THE BOOK AT US!

I'LL FIX IT SO THEY'LL NEVER THROW THE BOOK AT ME!

NEXT MORNING!

JACK!.. GUARD... HELP... HELP!

OH, GOD... WHY DID I EVER TAKE THAT FIRST REEFER! NOW I'LL NEVER BE ABLE TO STOP... I'LL WIND UP LIKE... LIKE HIM!

BUT YOU CAN STILL STOP, SON... MR. FORBES HERE IS FROM THE JUVENILE AID.

THE JUDGE HAS ALREADY PROMISED TO PAROLE YOU IN OUR CUSTODY, SON... IF YOU'LL PROMISE TO GO TO A FEDERAL HOSPITAL FOR SIX MONTHS! THEY'LL HELP YOU LICK THIS THING!

THE NEXT DAY...

GOOD-BY, SON... DO EVERYTHING THEY TELL YOU!

AND WHEN YOU COME BACK CURED, DARLING... I'LL BE WAITING FOR YOU!

ALL I WANT NOW IS GET THIS THING OUT OF MY SYSTEM! I USED TO THINK I COULD QUIT ANY TIME-- I'LL NEVER FALL INTO THAT TRAP AGAIN! DON'T WORRY, KATHY. I'LL STICK IT OUT!

16

The Opium Smugglers of Venus

FROM THE SENSUOUS THEATRE-WORLD OF THE *VENUS FREE STATE*, DOWN INTO THE MIASMIC JUNGLES OF THE VENUTIAN *TROPICS*, THE UNDAUNTED INTERPLANETARY SLEUTH PURSUES HIS ARCH-ENEMY, THE *MURDERER* FROM *MARS!* EVERY RESOURCE OF THE FAMOUS *AVENGER* IS NEEDED AS HE FIGHTS TO SOLVE THE WEIRD MYSTERY OF... *THE OPIUM SMUGGLERS' OF VENUS!*

A MOMENT LATER...

NARCOTICS FROM EARTH, ARE STILL BEING SMUGGLED INTO VENUS! SIRRAH VAU, OF THE GREBHAR CUSTOMS BUREAU, CONDEMNS OUR GOVERNMENT'S FAILURE TO STOP THE SMUGGLERS...

THIS COULD BE SOME NEW ACTIVITY OF MAAG'S! AVENGER AND TEENA SHOULD LOOK INTO THIS!

YOU BET!

NO ONE KNOWS THAT ROD HATHWAY AND HIS YOUNG SECRETARY ARE FAMOUS AVENGER AND TEENA. WITH A QUICK SWITCH INTO THEIR COSTUMES...

THERE'S THE VENUS EMBASSY! WE'LL INTERVIEW THIS SIRRAH VAU!

OUTSIDE THE EMBASSY...

SHH! THAT'S SIRRAH VAU! LISTEN!

YOU WILL BOOK PASSAGE ON THE *ARROW*, LEAVING TOMORROW! TAKE THIS MESSAGE TO THE SERENA VENTA!

WE'D BETTER TAKE A LOOK AT THAT MESSAGE!

RIGHT!

THIS ONE DROPPED THE LETTER! I'LL GET IT!

2

LET THEM GO! LET'S SEE THE LETTER!

IT'S IN THE VENUS LANGUAGE! WHAT'S IT SAY, AVENGER?

IT SAYS: VENTA, YOU FOOL! YOU'RE TAKING TOO MUCH OF THE STUFF! I'M DOING FINE! EARTH OFFICIALS ARE APOLOGIZING, BECAUSE THEY CAN'T CATCH THE SMUGGLERS!

BUT WHAT DO YOU FIGURE THAT LETTER MEANS?

THAT VENTA IS A DOPE ADDICT! AND I THINK SHE AND VAU BOTH ARE IN THIS SMUGGLING PLOT!

THEN PRESENTLY, IN THE EMBASSY...

WE THOUGHT WE'D GIVE YOU A LIFT ON THIS NARCOTICS SMUGGLING CASE, SIRRAH VAU!

WHY -- THAT IS KIND OF YOU, AVENGER!

I'M SURE YOU'LL ROUND UP THESE EARTH SMUGGLERS, AVENGER!

GOODBYE, SIRRAH!...

...TEENA, I WANTED TO TAKE A SECRET X-RAY OF HIM! I COULDN'T! HIS CLOTHES WERE IMPREGNATED WITH LEAD!

AND PRESENTLY, AVENGER'S LITTLE SPACE-FLYER, SWIFT AND POWERFUL, WINGS AWAY INTO THE NIGHT...

THAT ACTRESS, VENTA, WAS WITH MAAG, BOTH PASSENGERS ON THE STAR QUEEN, REMEMBER? AND WE NEVER SUSPECTED HER! WE'LL GO TO GREBHAR NOW AND SEE WHAT WE CAN LEARN FROM HER!

THEN AT LAST, SPREAD BENEATH THEM -- GREBHAR, GAY, BEAUTIFUL CAPITAL OF THE VENUS FREE STATE!

THE ARROW BEAT US IN! SHE'S JUST LANDING!

TONIGHT WE'LL GO TACKLE THAT VENTA WOMAN!

3

THAT EVENING...

TEENA, LOOK! THERE'S VENTA, ARRIVING AT THE STAGE ENTRANCE!

THAT'S VAU WITH HER! HE MUST HAVE JUST ARRIVED FROM EARTH ON THE *ARROW!*

HE'S GIVING HER A PACKAGE!

THAT DWARF IS ZORO! QUITE A FAMOUS DANCER HERE!

WEIRD STUFF, ISN'T IT!...THE LIVING DEAD--LIKE ZOMBIES!

THAT'S VENTA!

WITH THE BALLET STILL IN PROGRESS, AVENGER AND TEENA QUIETLY SLIP BACK-STAGE! AND IN VENTA'S DRESSING ROOM...

SHE'S GOT A BIG CACHE OF DRUGS HERE! VAU DELIVERS THE DRUGS TO HER--

AND HE SMUGGLES THEM FROM EARTH?

HE COULDN'T SMUGGLE DRUGS ON THE *ARROW!* PASSENGERS ARE TOO CAREFULLY SEARCHED! AND TEENA, THIS CONTAINER ISN'T OF EARTH MANUFACTURE! I DON'T THINK THE DRUGS ARE EITHER! IT'S ILLICIT STUFF, MADE HERE ON VENUS! THAT'S WHY HE BLAMED OUR EARTH OFFICIALS--JUST A COVER-UP!

THE FIRST ACT'S OVER! SHH! HERE COMES VENTA!

4

BUT WHERE IS TEENA? ALARMED AND PUZZLED, AVENGER DOESN'T SEE THE FIGURE BEHIND HIM, AND...

TEENA! WHERE ARE YOU, TEENA? UGH!

MEANWHILE...

QUIET NOW! IF YOU SCREAM, I KILL YOU!

OHHHH!

PRESENTLY...

NOT DEAD!

HE'S ALL RIGHT NOW!

TEENA! WHERE'S TEENA!

FRANTICALLY AVENGER SEARCHES! THEN AT LAST, AT A SECLUDED SIDE EXIT, BACKSTAGE...

...A MESSAGE? FROM TEENA?

TAKING ME 2°N 45°W

VISI-BOOTH

SUB-JET UPTOWN AND

SHE FOUND OUT WHERE THEY ARE TAKING HER AND WAS ABLE TO SCRAWL IT WITH A COSMETIC-STICK! THE LATITUDE AND LONGITUDE!

TAKING ME 2°N 45°W

A FEW MINUTES LATER...

GOT TO BORROW YOUR AIRCAR FOR A WHILE! I'LL RETURN IT AND PAY YOU WELL!

SOUTH INTO THE VENUS TROPICS, AVENGER SPEEDS! STEAMING, MIASMIC JUNGLE! AND THEN, AFTER FRANTIC HOURS OF SEARCH...

...A HIDDEN FACTORY WHERE THE NARCOTICS ARE MADE! VENUS POPPIES, BEING GROWN HERE! MAAG AND HIS SPACE BANDITS! MAKING THEIR GET-AWAY NOW-- BECAUSE THEY KNOW THEIR GAME IS UP!...

6

PRESENTLY, AS AVENGER GETS CLOSER...

YOU'LL MAKE A NICE HOSTAGE FOR ME, TEENA! I CAN BARGAIN WITH THE EARTH OFFICIALS-- THEY'LL BE WILLING TO RANSOM *YOU* FOR A FORTUNE OF PLATINUM INGOTS!

NOT IF I HAVE ANYTHING TO SAY ABOUT IT!

AVENGER!

THE WEIRD DUPLICATING RAY! AVENGER BATHES HIS FIGURE WITH IT, AND THE SPLITTING LIGHT-IMAGES OF HIM.

WHY--WHY-- WHICH ONE--?

WRONG GUESS, MAAG! HERE I AM!

HURRY AVENGER! WE'VE GOT TO GET AWAY FROM HERE!

THEY PLANTED AN H-BOMB TO DESTROY THEIR PLACE HERE! WE'VE GOT TO RUN!

FIGHTING WITH YOU DELAYED THEIR GETAWAY! THE-- BOMBS WILL GO OFF ANY SECOND!

WE MADE IT! WE'RE ALL RIGHT!

SO IS MAAG AND ALL HIS MURDEROUS CREW! BUT I'LL NEVER REST 'TILL I GET THEM, TEENA!

7

8

HOW THE NARCOTICS SQUAD GOT THE HOPPED-UP KILLER

WALLACE REAGAN WAS JUST ANOTHER SMALL TIME PUNK WITH BIG TIME IDEAS UNTIL THE FATEFUL DAY THAT HIS GUN MOLL INTRODUCED HIM TO THE HABIT OF BOLSTERING HIS NERVE WITH THE EVIL DRUG MARIHUANA. ARMED WITH THIS FALSE SUBSTITUTE FOR COURAGE, REAGAN TERRORIZED THREE STATES IN AN OUTBREAK OF VICIOUSNESS AND CRIME UNPARALLELED IN MODERN POLICE ANNALS. READ HIS TRUE STORY. THE EVIL CIGARETTES MADE HIM A COP-KILLER --- BUT IN THE END ---

DURING THAT WEEK, THE NARCOTICS SQUAD RAIDED EVERY DOPE JOINT FOR MILES AROUND, INCLUDING THE ONE WHERE GENEVA HAD BEEN BUYING THEIR REEFERS...

O.K., YOU RATS! YOU'RE ALL UNDER ARREST!

DROP THAT GUN!

WHAT THE... COPS! OWWWW!

NICE WORK, O'BRIAN. NOW I'D LIKE YOU TO LEAVE SOME STUFF AND A COUPLE OF MEN IN EVERY PLACE WE RAIDED. THAT COP KILLER CAN'T LIVE WITHOUT DOPE.

I'D LIKE TO STAY MYSELF, SIR. THE OFFICER THAT WAS KILLED WAS MY SISTER'S HUSBAND!

MEANWHILE: INFLAMED AND ENCOURGED BY GENEVA AND HER FAST DWINDLING SUPPLY OF DRUGS, REAGAN LED DUTCH EDDIE FROM ONE DESPERATE CRIME TO ANOTHER. EVEN HIS HARD-BOILED HENCHMEN WAS APPALLED AT REAGAN'S SADISTIC AND BLOOD-THIRSTY ACTS OF CRUELTY.

NOT THAT OLD LADY, WALLY!

SHUT UP! SHE COULD TURN US IN!

THE NARCOTICS SQUAD WAS READY TO WAIT WEEKS FOR THE TRAP TO WORK!

SCOTTY, YOUR PLAN HASN'T WORKED!

GIVE ME A COUPLE OF MORE DAYS. WITHOUT REEFERS THE GANG WILL GO CRAZY AND WALK INTO OUR TRAP!

WANTED

LATER... THAT DAY...

WE'RE OUT OF REEFERS, DUTCHY!

YEA! RUN OUT AND GET US SOME...!

NUTS, WALLY... I'M HOT... YOU'LL JUST HAVE TO GET ALONG WITHOUT THEM.

REAGAN WENT INSANE WITH RAGE WHEN HE FOUND HIMSELF FACED WITH LOSING HIS SUPPLY OF MARI-HUANA...

WHY YOU DOUBLE CROSSING RAT.. I'LL TEACH YOU TO CROSS ME...

5

6

THAT WAS O'BRIAN'S MISTAKE. HE BELIEVED THE HOP-HEAD...

YOU'LL NEVER TAKE ME ALIVE, COPPER!...UGGH!

WHY YOU-- ARHHH!

I GOT HIM...BUT I'M HIT BAD! WHERE CAN I GO? WHOM CAN I TRUST?

MEANWHILE: O'BRIANS PARTNER GAVE THE ALARM...

THERE. THAT SHOULD STOP THE BLEEDING...WHAT'S THAT? MORE COPS!

REAGAN WAS CORNERED LIKE A RAT. AND, LIKE A RAT, HE FOUGHT DESPERATELY. HE HELD OFF THE POLICE FOR HOURS, UNTIL...

IT...IT'S AWFULLY QUIET OUT THERE... WHAT'S GOING ON? WHAT'S THAT IN THE FAR CORNER?

DON'T TAKE ANY CHANCES UNTIL DAYLIGHT, MEN.

...HIS OWN DRUG STARVED BRAIN BETRAYED HIM! BRINGING THE NIGHTMARE VISIONS OF THE LAST STAGES OF ADDICTION...

GAHH! GO AWAY!

B'ZZM

YAHHH...LET ME OUT OF HERE!

NO! AAAAHHHHH!

GET HIM!

BAM

BAM

RATATAT

YES, A HOP-HEAD IS A KILLER— IF YOU GIVE HIM A BREAK, YOU'RE CRAZY-- I KNOW-- I WAS THE COP WHO KILLED HIM!

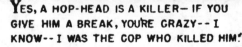

END

SUBSCRIBE TO "FIGHT AGAINST CRIME". 12 ISSUES $1.20. STORY COMICS INC., 7 E. 44TH. ST. N.Y. 17, N.Y.

MEN IN BLACK

by Stan Lee + Romita

A LIST OF ALL THE SINS OF WHICH MAN IS CAPABLE WOULD FILL VOLUMES MUCH THICKER THAN THIS ONE! BUT ONE OF THE MOST DANGEROUS OF ALL SINS IS *BIGOTRY!* THIS IS YOUR STORY, JIM HORTON...FOR YOU ARE A BIGOT!

I GOT FIRED TODAY! ME...A 100% AMERICAN... *FIRED!* AND THAT LOUSY IMMIGRANT WHO WORKS IN THAT DEPARTMENT IS STILL WORKING THERE!

RELAX, HORTON! YOU KNOW THAT GONZALES IS A HARDER WORKER THAN YOU...AND HE KNOWS *TWICE* AS MUCH ABOUT THE MACHINES!

A TALE OF MADDENING *MENACE!*

C-608

LISTEN TO 'IM! LISTEN TO LUIGI HERE! LISTEN TO HOW THESE DIRTY FOREIGNERS ALWAYS STICK UP FOR EACH OTHER!

ALL RIGHT, HORTON... BEAT IT! I DON'T WANNA HEAR THAT KIND'A TALK IN MY BAR...AND I DON'T WANNA SEE YOUR UGLY PUSS IN HERE ANY MORE!

SURE, REILLY...I'D HAVE EXPECTED YOU TO SAY THAT! YOU WEREN'T EVEN BORN HERE! YOU'RE AS BAD AS THE OTHERS!

BUT JUST WAIT... SOMEDAY US REAL AMERICANS'LL BAND TOGETHER AND PUT YOU ROTTEN CRUMBS WHERE YOU BELONG!

GET OUT... YOU'RE MAKIN' ME SICK!

1

YOU WALK DOWN THE STREET WITH YOUR MIND SEETHING! THE LIQUOR AND YOUR OWN BIGOTRY HAVE COMBINED TO MAKE YOUR THOUGHTS AS POISONOUS AND HATE-FILLED AS POSSIBLE!

THEY OUGHTTA BE KICKED OUTTA THIS COUNTRY...ALL OF 'EM...OR BETTER YET, WE OUGHTTA JUST ROUND 'EM UP AND MACHINE-GUN 'EM!

YOU SLAM OPEN THE DOOR OF YOUR RAMSHACKLE COTTAGE AND FIND YOURSELF CONFRONTED BY THE PATHETIC FIGURE OF MARION, YOUR WIFE...

I HEARD ABOUT IT, JIM! YOU GOT INTO A FIGHT WITH YOUR FOREMAN AND HE FIRED YOU!

YEAH, BUT WHAT ELSE CAN YA EXPECT FROM A CRUMMY FOREIGNER?

WELL, I'VE HAD ALL I CAN STAND OF YOU! I'M LEAVING, JIM... RIGHT NOW!

YOU CAN'T! I WON'T LET YOU! YOU'RE ALL I GOT!

YOU HAVEN'T GOT ME, JIM! YOU NEVER HAD ME! THERE WAS NEVER ROOM IN THAT HATE-RIDDEN HEART OF YOURS FOR ANY LOVE FOR ANYBODY!

IF YOU WANT TO GET IN TOUCH WITH ME FOR ANYTHING, CONTACT MY LAWYER! HE'LL KNOW WHERE TO REACH ME!

SURE...I MIGHT'VE KNOWN! IT'S PROBABLY ALL HIS FAULT! HE PROBABLY TALKED YOU INTO IT... I MIGHT'VE KNOWN THIS WOULD HAPPEN WITH A LAWYER NAMED GREENBERG!

JIM...TAKE MY ADVICE BEFORE I GO...SEE A DOCTOR...A GOOD DOCTOR...YOU'RE A SICK MAN, JIM... VERY SICK!

GO ON...GET OUT! I DON'T NEED ADVICE FROM YOU OR ANYBODY! I DON'T TRUST NONE OF YA! IT SERVES ME RIGHT FOR MARRYIN' A SWEDE!

AS THE DOOR SLAMS BEHIND HER, THE FINAL THREAD OF DECENCY SEEMS TO SNAP IN YOUR BRAIN! YOU CHARGE AROUND THE ROOM LIKE A CAGED BEAST...

THEY'VE GOTTA BE DRIVEN OUT! IT'S THEM OR US! I'LL KILL 'EM...I'LL KILL 'EM ALL! I'LL MAKE 'EM PAY FOR WHAT THEY DID TO ME!

CRASH

2

YOU LEAVE YOUR HOUSE AND START MAKING THE ROUNDS! YOU CONTACT YOUR PALS...HOODLUMS, LOAFERS, PETTY CROOKS, AND MALCONTENTS LIKE YOURSELF...

HEY, ROCKY! I WANNA SEE YA!

IN EVERY TOWN THERE ARE SOME MEN WHO'LL STOP AT NOTHING FOR A CHANCE TO TORTURE THOSE WHO ARE WEAKER THAN THEMSELVES! YOU'VE *FOUND* THOSE MEN!

PETE! WE'RE HAVIN' A MEETIN' T'NIGHT AT MY PLACE... NINE SHARP! BE THERE!

GOTCHA!

IT DOESN'T TAKE LONG! YOU HAVE EVERYTHING ORGANIZED BY 10 P.M.!

I'M FORMIN' A GANG! WE'RE GONNA WEAR BLACK SHEETS AND WE'RE GONNA RUN EVERY FOREIGNER OUTTA THIS TOWN!

WHAT'S IN IT FER US?

YEAH...WHAT'S OUR ANGLE?

WE GRAB EVERYTHING WE CAN FROM THESE DIRTY IMMIGRANTS! WE'LL BEAT 'EM AN' ROB 'EM! WE'LL SEND 'EM BACK WHERE THEY CAME FROM!

OKAY WITH ME... AS LONG AS THERE'LL BE ENOUGH LOOT!

I'M IN!

WHEN DO WE START?

THE NEXT NIGHT, ALL EIGHT OF YOU HAVE BLACK SHEETS ON... AND YOU HEAD FOR YOUR FIRST VICTIM...GONZALES!

HE LIVES IN THIS HOUSE! LET'S GO GET 'IM!

THIS OUGHTTA BE FUN!

CRASH

WHAT'S GOIN' ON? WHAT'S HAPPENING?

COME ON OUT, GONZALES! WE *WANT* YOU!

I'LL PHONE THE POLICE!

WHO ARE YOU? WHAT DO YOU WANT WITH ME?

WE WANNA TEACH YA A LESSON ABOUT FIRING REAL AMERICANS FROM THEIR JOBS!

AND THEN WE'RE GONNA BASH YOUR SKULL IN AS A WARNIN' TO OTHER STINKIN' FOREIGNERS!

3

WHY DO YOU CALL ME "FOREIGNER"? I'M AN AMERICAN CITIZEN! I...
UGH!

SHUT YER YAP, RAT!

HE'S OUT COLD!

SO WHAT? KEEP HITTIN' HIM! HE MIGHT'A RECOGNIZED MY VOICE... I WANNA MAKE SURE HE DON'T TALK!

LISTEN! THE COPS!

WOOOEEEEE

YOU REALIZE YOU MADE A MISTAKE! YOU GAVE SOMEONE IN THE HOUSE TIME TO PHONE THE COPS! BUT YOU WON'T MAKE A *SECOND* MISTAKE! YOU RUN...FAST!

LIFT 'EM... ALL OF YA!

ONE OF 'EM'S GETTING AWAY!

POLICE

YOU SOMEHOW MANAGE TO MAKE IT BACK TO YOUR ROOM! YOU SLAM THE DOOR BEHIND YOU...BREATHLESSLY!

MADE IT!

SLAM

YOU TAKE OFF THE BLACK SHEET IN PANIC...YOU'VE GOT TO HIDE IT...GOT TO DESTROY THE EVIDENCE!

I'LL BURN THE SHEET AN' PILLOWCASE...THEN NOBODY'LL BE ABLE TO PROVE NOTHIN'!

BUT...AS YOU LOOK IN THE MIRROR, YOU GASP IN TERROR...YOU'RE STILL WEARING A BLACK PILLOWCASE OVER YOUR HEAD...

I MUST BE GOIN' BATTY! I DON'T REMEMBER PUTTIN' ON *TWO* PILLOWCASES!

WITH CLUMSY, GROPING FINGERS YOU TEAR THE PILLOWCASE FROM YOUR HEAD...BUT...

ANOTHER ONE!

4

FEAR CLUTCHES YOUR HEART WITH ICY FINGERS AS YOU RIP THE BLACK HOOD FROM YOUR HEAD... BUT UNDER IT...

OH, NO! NO!

YOU GIVE WAY TO PANIC! YOU CAN'T BE FOUND WITH IT ON YOUR HEAD! YOU TEAR IT AS IF YOUR LIFE DEPENDED ON IT...

RRRIIIIIIIIPP!

HOW DID IT HAPPEN? WHERE DID THEY COME FROM?

NO MATTER HOW MANY I RIP OFF... THERE'S STILL ANOTHER ONE UNDERNEATH!

MAYBE YOU PUT THEM ON WHEN YOU WERE DRUNK... MAYBE YOU DID IT FOR A GAG... MAYBE YOU FORGOT...

GOTTA GET 'EM OFF! GOTTA GET 'EM OFF!

YOUR FINGERS REND AND TEAR AND SCRAPE AND RIP AND SLASH AND PULL AND GRIP AND SEVER AND SPLIT... YOU CAN THINK OF NOTHING ELSE... NOTHING BUT GETTING THOSE HORRIBLE BLACK HOODS OFF YOUR HEAD...

ARGGHH RRRIIIIIPPPP OHHH OHH

AND WHEN THE POLICE BREAK IN A FEW MINUTES LATER, THEY'RE MET BY A STRANGE AND GRUESOME SIGHT...

WHAT DO YOU MAKE OF IT, CHIEF?

BEATS ME, PAT! THERE'S HIS HOOD LYING ON THE FLOOR... BUT I CAN'T MAKE SENSE OUTTA IT.!..

LOOKS LIKE HE JUST TRIED TO RIP HIS FACE CLEAN OFF!

LIKE YOUR WIFE SAID, JIM, YOU WERE AN AWFULLY SICK MAN! BUT WHAT BIGOT ISN'T?

THE END

The MONSTER OF FRANKENSTEIN

SPEAK NO EVIL, SEE NO EVIL, HEAR NO EVIL-- THREE EVIL MEN ATTEMPTED TO APPLY THIS SAYING TO THE FRANKENSTEIN MONSTER. THEIR METHODS WERE CRUEL, BARBARIC AND WICKED. BUT IN THE END, THEY MET WITH...

THREE-FOLD HORROR and REVENGE!

THERE WERE THREE BROTHERS...JOHN, JAMES AND JEROME. EACH WAS A SUCCESSFUL ARTIST.

JOHN WAS A PAINTER. HIS EYES AND HIS VISION ENABLED HIM TO PAINT GREAT PICTURES.	JAMES WAS A SINGER. HIS VOICE BROUGHT HIM FAME AND WEALTH.	JEROME WAS A CONDUCTOR. THROUGH HIS EARS THE CONCERTS AND SYMPHONIES GAVE LIFE A MEANING TO HIM.

ONCE A YEAR THE BROTHERS TAKE A VACATION TOGETHER AND GO TO A CABIN IN THE WOODS. BUT IT IS ONLY A RETREAT FROM CITY LIFE, BECAUSE THEY STILL DO WHAT THEY LOVE TO DO.

JOHN PAINTS PICTURES...

JAMES SINGS TO HIS HEART'S CONTENT. HIS VOICE ECHOING AMONGST THE HILLS AND VALLEYS...

AND JEROME LISTENS ENDLESSLY TO PRECIOUS RECORDINGS, SEEKING NEW MEANING IN THE SYMPHONIES HE KNOWS SO WELL...

UNTIL ONE DAY JOHN HAS MADE A DISCOVERY AND HE EXCITEDLY TELLS HIS BROTHERS ABOUT IT!

A MONSTER! AN UNBELIEVABLY UGLY MONSTER! I FOUND HIM-- STUCK IN THE QUICKSAND IN THE BOG! COME QUICKLY!

THERE! THERE IT IS! WHAT DO YOU MAKE OF IT?

A LIVING HORROR! IT IS A BLIGHT UPON THE BEAUTY OF NATURE! IT DOES NOT DESERVE TO LIVE!

TRUE! THERE, CAUGHT IN THE QUICKSAND UP TO HIS NECK, THE FRANKENSTEIN MONSTER IS MORE HELPLESS THAN HE HAS EVER BEEN!

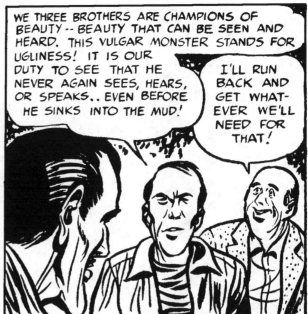

3

THE MONSTER IS HELPLESS AS JEROME SEALS HIS LIPS FOREVER.

JAMES USES HIS IMPLEMENTS, AND THE MONSTER WILL NEVER HEAR...

JOHN BLOTS THE VISION OUT OF THE MONSTER'S EYES...

WHEW -- THAT'S THAT! WE HAVE DONE OUR PART IN DESTROYING UGLINESS!

I MUST ADMIT IT IS PRETTY HORRIBLE -- BUT HE WILL BE DEAD IN A SHORT WHILE.

YES, HE'LL BE DEAD. HE WILL SINK DOWN IN THE MUD OVER HIS HEAD AND WILL ROT THERE AND NOBODY WILL BE THE WISER!

LET'S GET BACK TO THE CABIN. I NEED A GOOD DRINK!

SPEAK NO EVIL, SEE NO EVIL, HEAR NO EVIL. THAT WRETCH WE LEFT IN THE BOG IS THOSE THREE MONKEYS ROLLED UP INTO ONE!

SPEAK, SEE, HEAR --- NEVER AGAIN WILL THE FRANKENSTEIN MONSTER DO ANY OF THESE.

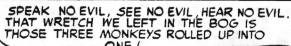

4

SO THE MONSTER IS LEFT TO SINK! BUT HE DOESN'T SINK ANY FURTHER! HIS FEET HIT SOMETHING SOLID AND HE REMAINS WITH HIS HEAD ABOVE THE MUD... UNTIL ...

HURRYING OFF, THE OLD CRONE GOES TO A FRIEND SHE CAN TRUST...

QUICKLY, TORG... BRING YOUR HORSE AND CHAINS AND DO WHAT I SAY! AND ABOVE ALL, TELL NO ONE OF WHAT HAPPENS!

THE CHAIN IS PUT AROUND THE MONSTER'S NECK, THE ONLY PLACE IT CAN HOLD TO! THE OLD CRONES HOPE IT WILL HOLD! THE HORSE PULLS...

SLOWLY THE BODY SLIPS FROM THE HUGGING MUD! ANOTHER CHAIN IS SLIPPED UNDER HIS ARMS...

AND SOON, THE FRANKENSTEIN MONSTER IS BEING LED AWAY BY THE OLD HAG!

HMM! IT LOOKS LIKE YOU'RE IN BAD SHAPE! BUT THAT DOESN'T DISCOURAGE ME! YOU STAY HERE, AND I'LL TAKE CARE OF YOU! MY BREWS AND POTIONS WILL WORK WONDERS ON YOUR WOUNDS!

I DON'T KNOW HOW LONG IT WILL TAKE, BUT SOME DAY YOU'LL BE GOOD AS NEW! YOU'LL BE ABLE TO SEE AND HEAR LIKE ANYBODY ELSE! SURE... IT'S ALL IN MY SECRET POTIONS!

WEEKS LATER, AFTER THE OLD HAG TREATS THE MONSTER WITH HER SPECIAL METHODS AND MYSTERIOUS HOMEMADE MEDICINES...

AH! SO YOU CAN HEAR NOW. FINE! SOON YOU'LL BE AS WELL AS YOU'VE EVER BEEN!

AND IN THE COURSE OF TWO MONTHS, THE FRANKENSTEIN MONSTER ONCE AGAIN CAN SEE AND HEAR! HE IS ALL WELL... AS IF NOTHING HAPPENED... EXCEPT THAT HE REMEMBERS MOST VIVIDLY THE ACTIONS OF THOSE THREE MEN THAT AWFUL DAY!

FOOD! LOTS OF FOOD FOR BOTH OF US!

WHAT ARE YOU STARING AT? THAT'S ONLY THE NEWSPAPER I USED TO WRAP THE FOOD IN!

MUSIC AND ART BROTHERS

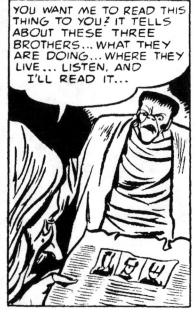

YOU WANT ME TO READ THIS THING TO YOU? IT TELLS ABOUT THESE THREE BROTHERS... WHAT THEY ARE DOING... WHERE THEY LIVE... LISTEN, AND I'LL READ IT...

THE MONSTER LISTENS! HE FINDS OUT WHERE HE CAN FIND EACH OF THESE THREE ENEMIES OF HIS! AND THEN... HE IS OFF... FOR A TERRIBLE REVENGE!

JOHN IS IN THIS STUDIO, PAINTING! HE, LIKE HIS BROTHERS, HAS ALMOST FORGOTTEN ABOUT HOW THEY TORTURED THE MONSTER WHOM HE THINKS BY NOW IS A DECOMPOSED MASS AT THE BOTTOM OF A QUICKSAND PIT...

6

SUDDENLY THERE IS A TREMENDOUS CRASH AS THE FRANKENSTEIN MONSTER PLUNGES THROUGH THE SKYLIGHT...

YOU! NO! IT--IT'S IMPOSSIBLE! I MYSELF BLINDED YOU MONTHS AGO--- LEFT YOU TO SINK IN THE MUD--- HOW ?? NO, DON'T!

WITH TWO FINGERS OF STEELY STRENGTH OUTSTRETCHED, THE MONSTER ADVANCES UPON HIS ENEMY!

YAARGG

I'M BLIND! BLIND! EVERY-THING IS BLACK! I CAN'T SEE! MY PAINTINGS--- I'LL NEVER SEE THEM AGAIN! YAAAHH!

BLIND--CAN'T SEE... I'D RATHER BE DEAD--- NEVER TO SEE AGAIN...!!

IN HIS HOME, JEROME IS LISTENING TO HIS PRECIOUS RECORDS ON HIS ELABORATE SOUND SYSTEM...

WHAT? NO!! IT CAN'T BE! YOU'RE DEAD! YOU SHOULD BE DEAD!! WH--WHAT ARE YOU GOING TO DO?

7

There is a loud crunch as both his hands come together quickly and sharply upon Jerome's ears!

And when he regains consciousness the monster is gone, and Jerome remembers nothing!

Jerome's snapped mind can't realize that his eardrums are broken, and that he's completely deaf!

In another part of town, James is giving a concert. He has never sung better in his life...

Suddenly from far above, a rope falls to the stage next to James. Though confused, he continues singing...

8

WITH GREAT SPEED FOR HIS GREAT SIZE, THE MONSTER MAKES HIS WAY DOWN THE SIDE OF THE BUILDING . . .

THERE HE GOES! AFTER HIM BEFORE HE GETS AWAY!

THERE IS ONLY ONE ESCAPE--OFF THE BRIDGE INTO THE WATER. THE MONSTER DIVES . . .

HE IS GONE--WE'VE EITHER LOST HIM OR HE'S STILL UNDER THE WATER--IN WHICH CASE HE'S SURE TO BE DROWNED BY NOW!

SOMETIME LATER, IN AN INSANE ASYLUM . . .

WHAT A LOSS TO THE WORLD OF ART AND MUSIC. THE BROTHERS ARE COMPLETELY INSANE. THEY SIT AROUND LIKE STATUES ALL DAY . . .

YES, THEY DO RESEMBLE A STATUE--THE STATUE OF THE THREE WISE MONKEYS . . . SPEAK NO EVIL, SEE NO EVIL AND HEAR NO EVIL!

THE END

THIS ISN'T A HAPPY TALE... IT'S THE TRAGIC STORY OF HOW A MAN BECAME TRAPPED BY A FLAW IN HIS CHARACTER! THIS HAPPENED TO MY BROTHER BUT IT COULD HAPPEN TO YOU OR ANY BODY ELSE WHO IS...

GUN HAPPY

BLAM!

FROM THE TIME TOM WAS A LITTLE BOY IN "NEW TOWN" MAINE, HE ALWAYS LOVED GUNS, NOT JUST ADMIRED THEM, BUT LOVED THEM

GEE, BILL, AREN'T THESE THE PRETTIEST GUNS YOU'VE EVER SEEN?

YES, THEY ARE PRETTY ALRIGHT!

YOU KNOW TOM, I'VE BEEN THINKING IT OVER, WHEN I GROW UP, I WANT TO BE A POLICEMAN!

THAT'S ONE WAY OF GETTING GUNS, BUT IT'S TOO SLOW AND IT TAKES TOO LONG!

WHEN TOM WAS FIFTEEN..

I CAN'T WAIT ANY LONGER, I'VE GOT TO HAVE A GUN! NOBODY'S AROUND, HERE GOES...

GUN AND SPORTING GOODS

CRASH

HALT! HALT OR I'LL SHOOT!!

HE WAS CAUGHT AND...

THOMAS PARKER, I HEREBY SENTENCE YOU TO THREE YEARS IN THE REFORM SCHOOL...

THE YEARS DRAGGED BY AND FINALLY HE WAS RELEASED! HE JOINED THE ARMY TO BE NEAR HIS ONE LOVE... GUNS...

THIS ONE'S MINE--ALL MINE! SHINE FOR PAPA, BABY!

WHEN YOU LOVE SOMETHING, YOU GET GOOD AT IT--TOM SOON WAS THE BEST SHOT IN HIS COMPANY...

PARKER, YOU'RE THE BEST SHOT I'VE EVER SEEN! A NATURAL BORN MARKSMAN! MY SISTER IS THE ONLY OTHER PERSON I KNOW OF WHOSE SHOOTING APPROACHES YOURS...

I LOVE TO SHOOT GUNS, SARGE!

BAM!

WELL, THE TWO MEN BECAME BUDDIES, AND SERGEANT CRAWFORD WAS ALWAYS TELLING TOM ABOUT HIS SISTER ANN...

...THAT'S RIGHT, TOM--SHE'S WON EVERY SHOOTING MATCH AND TURKEY SHOOT WE'VE EVER HELD! NOW SHE'S WORKING AS A TESTER IN THE MANCHESTER ARMS CO. BACK HOME!

THE TWO BUDDIES WERE SEPARATED FOREVER ON "OLD BALDY" IN KOREA...

YOU...MUST PROMISE... ME...TOM...TO SEE ANN FOR...ME...PROMISE TOM....

I PROMISE, BOB...BOB! BOB!!

2

AFTER TOM WAS DISCHARGED, HE LOOKED UP BOB'S SISTER IN CONNECTICUT...

YOU'RE JUST LIKE BOB'S LETTERS SAID YOU WERE! I'M HAPPY TO MEET YOU, TOM!

I'VE BEEN LOOKING FORWARD TO THIS FOR A LONG TIME!

IT WAS LOVE AT FIRST SIGHT, AND AFTER 2 MONTHS...

ANN DARLING... I LOVE YOU...

TOM, OH TOM...

THE CEREMONY WAS SHORT AND SWEET...

...YOUR LAWFUL WEDDED WIFE?

I DO!

THE TWO WEEK FLORIDA HONEYMOON WAS A BINGE OF HIGH LIVING! ALL OF TOM'S BACK PAY AND ANN'S SMALL SAVINGS WERE SOON TO BE EXHAUSTED...

WE'RE BROKE, HONEY -- THE HONEYMOON'S OVER! TOMORROW, I HAVE TO FIND A JOB!

WHY SHOULD THE HONEYMOON EVER END? WHY SHOULD YOU PLUG AWAY FOR PEANUTS WHEN THERE'S AN EASIER WAY?

YOU MEAN... STEAL?

3

WHY NOT? WE HAVE OUR GUNS! WHY LIVE LIKE DIRT IF WE CAN LIVE LIKE KINGS? YOU'RE **NOT AFRAID**?

NO, TOM WAS NOT AFRAID AND SOON...

MARKSMAN KILLERS ROB BANK!!!

MR. & MRS. DEADEYE STRIKE AGAIN FOUR SHOT

THINGS WERE GOING THEIR WAY AND THEY WORKED ALL THE WAY BACK UP THE EAST COAST LEAVING A BLOODY TRAIL BEHIND THEM UNTIL ONE DAY...

MY HAND!! THEY CLIPPED MY HAND! QUICK, ANN, LET'S GO!

POW!

BANK

WE'VE GOT TO HOLE UP SOMEWHERE, ANN! I CAN'T STAND THE PAIN ANY LONGER...

TOM, WE'RE NEAR YOUR HOME-TOWN. IF WE TRY CRASHING THROUGH THE ROAD BLOCK, WE'LL NEVER GET THROUGH! HOW ABOUT HEADING FOR YOUR MOTHER'S PLACE?

MRS. PARKER, YOU'VE GOT TO HELP HIM! IT'S TOM, YOUR SON!

QUICK, GET INTO THE HOUSE! MY POOR BOY!

IN TWO WEEKS TOM'S HAND HAD HEALED! ONE DAY...

ANN, A CAR IS STOPPING IN FRONT OF THE HOUSE!

I KNEW WE SHOULDN'T HAVE LET YOUR MOTHER GO OUT!

4

MOTHER HAD COME TO ME AND TOLD ME THE WHOLE STORY! SHE FELT SHE HAD TO HELP TOM WHILE HE WAS HURT, BUT NOW SHE MUST DO WHAT WAS RIGHT BY THE LAW, SO SHE TURNED TO ME...

COME IN, BILL!

HELLO, TOM!

I'M YOUR BROTHER, AND I HAVE TO TAKE YOU IN, TOM! PLEASE DON'T DO ANYTHING FOOLISH!

KILL HIM, TOM! KILL HIM AND LET'S BLOW, FAST!

SHUT UP, ANN! HE'S MY OWN BROTHER! I CAN'T SHOOT HIM! GIVE ME A ROPE!

WHAT GOOD WILL THAT DO? MY MEN KNOW I'M HERE! IF I'M NOT BACK IN AN HOUR, THEY WILL COME HERE!

ALRIGHT, SO THEY FIND YOU! IN ONE HOUR, I'LL BE MILES AWAY FROM HERE! I'M SORRY TO PART LIKE THIS, BILL, I SHOULD HAVE TAKEN YOUR ADVICE WHEN WE WERE KIDS, BUT IT'S TOO LATE NOW!

WHERE ARE WE GOING? THIS LOOKS LIKE THE COUNTRY!

IT IS! THIS IS LIZARD SWAMP. I PLAYED HERE WHEN I WAS A KID! I KNOW EVERY ROCK AND TREE! I'LL DITCH THE CAR AND WE CAN HIDE HERE TILL MORNING! THEN WE CAN WALK INTO THE NEXT TOWN AND HOP A FREIGHT!

BACK IN NEWTOWN, I WAS PLANNING A WAY TO TRAP MY OWN BROTHER...

THERE'S ONLY ONE PLACE HE COULD GO WITHOUT RUNNING INTO A ROAD-BLOCK... LIZARD SWAMP! WE'LL GO OUT THERE AND BLOCK OFF ALL THE EXITS! IN THE MORNING, WE'LL CLOSE IN, BUT REMEMBER... NO SHOOTING UNLESS THEY START IT!

BY DAWN WE WERE READY TO CLOSE IN...

SHERIFF! THERE, THEY'RE IN THERE!

5

TOM, GIVE UP! IT'S ME, BILL! WE HAVE YOU SURROUNDED! NO ONE WILL SHOOT IF YOU COME OUT WITH YOUR HANDS UP!

DON'T DO IT, TOM! I'M NOT AFRAID TO DIE, BUT NOT IN THE ELECTRIC CHAIR! LET'S FIGHT IT OUT!

NO, I'M TIRED OF KILLING!

REMEMBER, TOM, DON'T SHOOT! THESE MEN WILL CUT THAT SWAMP TO PIECES! COME OUT WITH YOU HANDS UP!

IT'S ALL OVER, ANN! LET'S GIVE OURSELVES UP!

I CAN'T GIVE UP, TOM! I CAN'T!

ANN-- NO! DON'T!

I'M SORRY, ANN, BUT I CAN'T LET YOU SHOOT MY OWN BROTHER!

BAM!

BE BRAVE, DEAR! IT WILL SOON BE OVER! GOODBYE!

NO, TOM! NO!!

THEN TOM FIRED AGAIN--INTO THE AIR! WELL, THE DEPUTIES AND TROOPERS DIDN'T KNOW THAT HE COULD HAVE SHOT ANYONE OF US WITH NO TROUBLE AT THAT RANGE AND SO...

SO, THEY WANT TO SHOOT IT OUT, EH? OPEN FIRE!

RAT-TA-TA-TA--

BAM! BAM! BAM!

...AND SO WE FOUND THEM! ANN AND MY BROTHER, MY GUN HAPPY BROTHER!

THE END

"IT'S BEST TO KNOW"

...about alcohol

"ALCOHOL MEANS MANY THINGS TO MANY PEOPLE... THE QUESTION IS, WILL ALCOHOL CONTROL US OR WILL WE CONTROL ALCOHOL?"

IN THE EARLIEST TIMES IT WAS CUSTOMARY FOR MAN TO DRAW HIS OWN BLOOD AND MINGLE IT WITH ANOTHER'S BLOOD AS A SIGN OF TRUST AND FRIENDSHIP

STONE AGE BLOOD BROTHERS

ELIZABETHAN BUSINESSMEN

LATER ON, A CUP OF WINE OR OTHER ALCOHOLIC DRINK WAS USED TO SEAL AGREEMENTS. IT WAS CALLED "AQUA VITAE" (WATER OF LIFE), AND IT BECAME IDENTIFIED WITH BLOOD, "THE STREAM OF LIFE."

THIS "STREAM OF LIFE" SYMBOLISM HAS GIVEN TO ALCOHOLIC BEVERAGES A PRESTIGE WHICH EXPLAINS THEIR WIDE ACCEPTANCE IN MANY PARTS OF THE WORLD DOWN THROUGH THE AGES.

ON SAILING SHIPS A TOT OF RUM WAS ISSUED AFTER THE DIFFICULT JOB OF SPLICING THE MAINBRACE. IN THE NAVY TODAY THERE IS AN ORDER TO "SPLICE THE MAINBRACE" RESERVED FOR SPECIAL OCCASIONS.

WEDDINGS HAVE LONG BEEN OCCASIONS FOR TOASTS TO THE NEWLY-WEDS IN MANY PARTS OF THE WORLD . . . . .

OFFERING A DRINK TO ONE'S GUEST IS A SYMBOL OF HOSPITALITY IN MANY PLACES TODAY . . . . . *

*NOTE: THE GOOD HOST OR HOSTESS WILL OFFER ALTERNATIVES TO THE ALCOHOLIC DRINKS, FOR NON-DRINKERS

HISTORY SHOWS THAT PEOPLE HAVE TRIED TO PREVENT INTEMPERATE USE OF ALCOHOL.....

IN ANCIENT BABYLON (ABOUT 2225 B.C.) KING HAMMURABI SET UP THE OLDEST KNOWN SYSTEM OF CODIFIED LAW, AND SEVERAL SECTIONS WERE DEVOTED TO PROBLEMS CREATED BY THE ABUSE OF ALCOHOLIC BEVERAGES.

HAMMURABI AS A JUDGE
(RELIEF TABLET IN LOUVRE)

IN CHINA, LAWS THAT FORBADE MAKING WINE WERE ENACTED AND REPEALED FORTY-ONE TIMES FROM 1100 B.C. TO 1400 A.D.

IN NORTH AMERICA, PROHIBITION DURING THE 1920'S WAS ACCOMPANIED BY GOOD AND BAD RESULTS: A REDUCTION IN PER CAPITA CONSUMPTION AND ALCOHOLISM ON ONE HAND, A RISE IN LAWLESSNESS ON THE OTHER.

THERE ARE THREE BASIC KINDS OF ALCOHOLIC BEVERAGES . . . . .

BEER IS PRODUCED BY ALLOWING A BROTH MADE FROM CEREAL GRAINS TO FERMENT UNDER CONTROLLED CONDITIONS.

. . . SOME EUROPEAN COUNTRIES HAVE TAKEN GREAT PRIDE IN THE ART OF BREWING.

STONE AGE BEER JUGS HAVE BEEN UNEARTHED, INDICATING THAT BREWED DRINKS WERE KNOWN AS FAR BACK AS THE NEOLITHIC PERIOD. . . . .

WASSERBURG ON LAKE CONSTANCE, GERMANY

WINE IS PRODUCED BY THE NATURAL FERMENTATION OF GRAPES OR OTHER FRUIT . . . . .

IN ITALY WINE IS TAKEN CHIEFLY AT MEALTIME. DRUNKENNESS IS FROWNED UPON AS A SIGN OF IMMATURITY . . . .

IN FRANCE WINE IS DRUNK THROUGHOUT THE DAY. ABSTINENCE IS GENERALLY FROWNED UPON, AND ALCOHOLISM IS WIDESPREAD.

SPIRITS ARE PRODUCED BY DISTILLING A FERMENTED BREW MADE FROM CEREAL GRAINS, MOLASSES OR FROM WINE.

... IN NORTH AMERICA HARD DRINKING WAS A PART OF PIONEER LIFE.

TODAY MANY TRY TO APPEAR MORE GROWN UP BY "DRINKING LIKE A MAN."

ALCOHOL BOILS AT A LOWER TEMPERATURE THAN WATER AND VAPORIZES, SO WHEN FERMENTED BREWS (MOSTLY ALCOHOL AND WATER) ARE HEATED THE ALCOHOL IS VAPORIZED FIRST. BY PASSING THIS VAPOR THROUGH A COOLING TUBE IT IS CHANGED BACK TO A LIQUID THAT IS ABOUT HALF ALCOHOL. THIS IS HOW SPIRITS ARE DISTILLED. . . . . .

VAPOUR

COOLING TUBE

TO LIQUID

VAPOUR

FERMENTED BREW

ALCOHOL

DRINK CHART

HERE IS HOW THE DIFFERENT KINDS OF ALCOHOLIC DRINKS COMPARE IN TERMS OF ALCOHOLIC CONTENT

 =  =

1½ OZ. WHISKEY

3 OZ. PORT OR SHERRY

12 OZ. BEER

ALCOHOL NEEDS NO DIGESTING AND IS ABSORBED DIRECTLY THROUGH THE WALLS OF THE STOMACH AND SMALL INTESTINE INTO THE BLOODSTREAM

OUR BODIES ARE ⅔ WATER

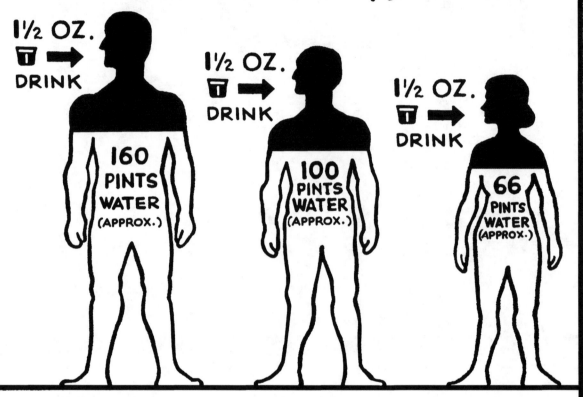

1½ OZ. DRINK →
160 PINTS WATER (APPROX.)

1½ OZ. DRINK →
100 PINTS WATER (APPROX.)

1½ OZ. DRINK →
66 PINTS WATER (APPROX.)

240 lb. MAN IS APPROX. 160 lbs. WATER

150 lb. MAN IS APPROX. 100 lbs. WATER

100 lb. WOMAN IS APPROX. 66 lbs. WATER

THE CONCENTRATION OF ALCOHOL, AND THEREFORE ITS EFFECT, VARIES WITH THE SIZE OF THE PERSON.

FOOD IN THE STOMACH SLOWS DOWN THE ABSORPTION OF ALCOHOL AND CONSEQUENTLY SLOWS DOWN THE RATE OF INTOXICATION. FATIGUE AND EMOTIONAL STATE ALSO MAY HAVE EFFECTS.

8 BOTTLES OF BEER

SIGNS TO NOTICE:
- STAGGERING
- LOSS OF BALANCE
- SEEING DOUBLE

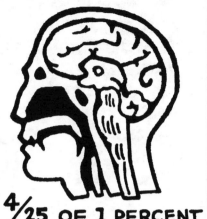

BLOOD-ALCOHOL LEVEL

$\frac{4}{25}$ OF 1 PERCENT

20 BOTTLES OF BEER

SIGNS TO NOTICE:
- SKIN IS CLAMMY
- PUPILS ARE DILATED
- UNCONSCIOUSNESS, OR "OUT LIKE A LIGHT."

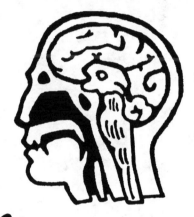

BLOOD-ALCOHOL LEVEL

$\frac{2}{5}$ OF 1 PERCENT

26 BOTTLES OF BEER

- DEATH DUE TO ALCOHOLIC POISONING

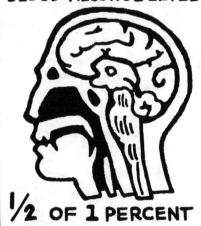

BLOOD-ALCOHOL LEVEL

$\frac{1}{2}$ OF 1 PERCENT

THESE ARE **AVERAGE** EFFECTS, ASSUMING THAT DRINKS ARE TAKEN FAIRLY QUICKLY.

WHEN ALCOHOL IS DISTRIBUTED THROUGHOUT THE BODY IN THE BLOODSTREAM, PART OF IT (ABOUT TWO PERCENT) IS ELIMINATED IN THE BREATH AND IN THE URINE. THE REST MUST BE BURNED IN THE BODY LIKE FATS, SUGARS AND OTHER FOODS. ONLY THE LIVER CAN BURN ALCOHOL, AND THIS AT A FIXED RATE. THUS, ALCOHOL IS PROCESSED MORE SLOWLY THAN OTHER FOODSTUFFS.

THIS CHART INDICATES HOW LONG IT TAKES ALCOHOL TO LEAVE THE BODY AND REDUCE ALCOHOL-BLOOD LEVEL TO A SAFE .03 PERCENT (3/100 OF 1 PERCENT).

AFTER THIS MANY DRINKS OF WHISKEY, BRANDY OR GIN, ETC.	IT TAKES THIS MANY HOURS FOR BODY TO BURN ALCOHOL *							
	1	2	3	4	5	6	7	8
🥃 (SEE DRINK CHART PAGE 9)								
🥃🥃	■	■						
🥃🥃🥃	■	■	■	■				
🥃🥃🥃🥃	■	■	■	■	■	■		
🥃🥃🥃🥃🥃	■	■	■	■	■	■	■	■

* DRIVERS SHOULD WAIT THIS MANY HOURS BEFORE THEY DRIVE CARS....

HOW LONG DOES INTOXICATION PERSIST....?

HOW LONG A PERSON STAYS DRUNK VARIES FROM ONE PERSON TO ANOTHER, AND DEPENDS PRIMARILY ON HOW MUCH A PERSON HAS DRUNK AND OVER WHAT PERIOD OF TIME.

HANGOVER USUALLY OCCURS BETWEEN FOUR TO TWELVE HOURS AFTER THE PEAK BLOOD-ALCOHOL LEVEL HAS BEEN PASSED.....

MOST COMMERCIAL AIRLINES PROHIBIT PILOTS FROM FLYING FOR 24 HOURS AFTER DRINKING ALCOHOL, TO BE SAFE !

DOES ALCOHOL ITSELF HARM THE DIGESTIVE TRACT ?

.. EXCESSIVE DRINKING OF STRAIGHT LIQUOR OFTEN PRODUCES INFLAMMATION OF THE STOMACH LINING, KNOWN AS "ALCOHOLIC GASTRITIS..." IT CAN BE PAINFUL AND SOMETIMES BLEEDING OCCURS.

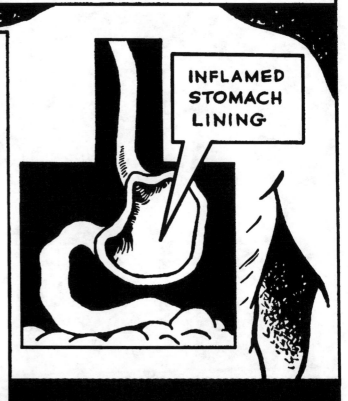

INFLAMED STOMACH LINING

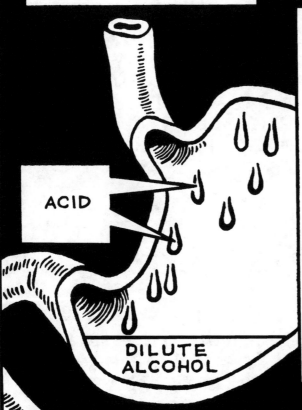

ACID

DILUTE ALCOHOL

.. DILUTE ALCOHOL DOES STIMULATE FORMATION OF ACID BY THE STOMACH, BUT THERE IS NO EVIDENCE TO SHOW THAT IT CAUSES STOMACH ULCERS. IN FACT, MODERATE QUANTITIES OF ALCOHOL MAY HELP TO PREVENT ULCERS IN SOME CASES BY REDUCING TENSION....

WHAT ABOUT ALCOHOL AS FOOD OR MEDICINE ?

NUTRITIONALLY ALCOHOL RESEMBLES PURE FAT OR STARCH IN THAT IT SUPPLIES ONLY CALORIES. IF IT REPLACES TOO MUCH OF A NORMAL DIET THE RESULTING IMBALANCE MAY LEAD TO MALNUTRITION....

ALCOHOL CONTAINS NONE OF THE ESSENTIAL VITAMINS, MINERALS OR AMINO ACIDS SO NECESSARY IN THE DAILY DIET, BUT IT CAN MAKE ONE FAT !

FOR EXAMPLE :

8 OZ. BEER	= 105 CALORIES	
1½ " GIN	= 105	"
1½ " RUM	= 105	"
1½ " WHISKEY	= 105	"
2 " PORT	= 106	"
2 " SHERRY	= 76	"

2 BEERS

CONTAIN MORE CALORIES THAN A PIECE OF PIE,

A CREAM PUFF,

OR A CANDY BAR ....

ALCOHOL'S MEDICINAL VALUE HAS BEEN OVERRATED IN THE PAST. TODAY IT IS SOMETIMES USED IN SMALL AMOUNTS AS A SEDATIVE.

IS ALCOHOL MORE DANGEROUS FOR YOUNG PEOPLE ?

ALCOHOL WORKS THE SAME WAY IN THE BODIES OF CHILDREN, ADOLESCENTS AND ADULTS (ALTHOUGH, OF COURSE, THE SAME AMOUNT OF ALCOHOL IN A SMALLER BODY HAS A LARGER EFFECT).

BUT PEOPLE ARE NOT THE SAME EMOTIONALLY AND THEREFORE REACT DIFFERENTLY.

UNCONTROLLED BEHAVIOUR BECAUSE OF INTOXICATION IS THE MAJOR HAZARD FOR YOUNG PEOPLE.

THIS IS A STORY OF WHAT MIGHT HAPPEN ANYWHERE.—EVEN RIGHT IN YOUR HOME TOWN. ITS MESSAGE IS ONE THAT EVERY GIRL AND BOY SHOULD REMEMBER...

THAT'S IT FOR TODAY, GUYS. TIME TO QUIT!

AND I'M READY. THIS HAS BEEN A LONG WORKOUT!

HI! WHAT'S WITH YOU GUYS? YOU LOOK BUSHED!

YEAH, WE OUGHT TO. WE'VE BEEN AT THE PLAYGROUND SINCE RIGHT AFTER SCHOOL!

WHAT YOU NEED IS A LIFT... SOME UPS OR SOMETHING. THEY KEEP YOU FROM RUNNING OUT OF GAS!

UPS? WHAT ARE UPS?

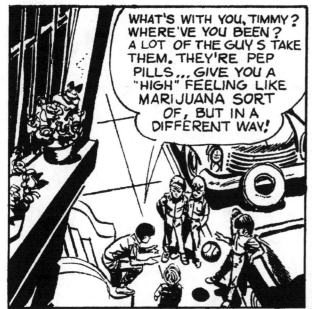

"THE STRONGER HALLUCINOGENS --
ESPECIALLY **LSD** -- CAN CAUSE A PERSON
TO BE DEPRESSED AND MENTALLY DIS-
TURBED FOR MONTHS OR YEARS AND
TO REQUIRE PSYCHIATRIC TREATMENT."

GEE, I DIDN'T KNOW DRUGS COULD DO THAT!

YES, TIMMY, IT'S SAD BUT TRUE
THAT MANY YOUNG PEOPLE ARE
RECEIVING MEDICAL TREATMENT
TODAY BECAUSE MONTHS AGO
THEY MADE THE MISTAKE OF
FOOLING AROUND WITH POWER-
FUL DRUGS LIKE **LSD**. SOME
FOUND IT SO
UNBEARABLE
THEY COMMITTED
SUICIDE.

BUT DAD, SOME OF THE MOST
POPULAR GIRLS I KNOW SMOKE
"POT" -- THAT'S WHAT THEY CALL
MARIJUANA, NOW TAKE BONNIE...
SHE'S SO POPULAR I ALMOST WISH
I COULD BE LIKE HER...

"... AT OUR LAST SCHOOL DANCE WHEN WE WERE
IN THE POWDER ROOM BONNIE TOOK A FEW PUFFS
OF A MARIJUANA CIGARETTE AND OFFERED IT TO
ME. SHE SAID IT WOULD MAKE ME LET GO AND GET
WITH IT -- HAVE A BALL! I DIDN'T SMOKE IT BUT SHE
WAS REALLY LIVING IT UP AND I'M CURIOUS ABOUT
WHAT IT WOULD HAVE DONE FOR ME..."

YES, IT'S CURIOSITY
THAT CAUSES A LOT
OF THE DRUG PROB-
LEMS, SUSAN --
A VERY DANGEROUS
PART. NO ONE EVER
STARTS OUT USING
DRUGS WANTING TO
GET HOOKED OR TO
BECOME DEPEND-
ENT ON THEM. BUT
THAT'S THE TROU-
BLE -- THAT FIRST
TIME CAN LEAD
TO A SECOND,
THEN TO A THIRD
AND THEN... WELL,
WHO KNOWS?

THE TROUBLE IS, ALMOST ALL THE ABUSED DRUGS CAN CAUSE A PERSON TO IMAGINE HE NEEDS THEM JUST TO HANDLE THE LITTLE EVERY DAY PROBLEMS THAT EVERYONE HAS TO FACE. THIS IS KNOWN AS "PSYCHOLOGICAL DEPENDENCE" AND CAN RESULT IN A HABIT AWFULLY HARD TO BREAK!

OH! THE DOORBELL! WHO COULD THAT BE HERE AT DINNER TIME?

I'LL GET THE DOOR!

HI, TIMMY! HI, MOM... DAD... SUSAN. I THOUGHT I'D SURPRISE YOU!

WHY, GARY, WHAT ARE YOU DOING HOME FROM COLLEGE? IS SOMETHING WRONG?

HOW COULD THERE BE WITH A SMILE LIKE THAT ON HIS FACE?

WHAT'S THIS SURPRISE VISIT ALL ABOUT, SON?

OUR BASEBALL TEAM PLAYS CENTRAL STATE HERE TOMORROW AND I'M PITCHING. IT'LL BE MY LAST GAME BEFORE GRADUATING. THE TEAM'S IN TOWN TONIGHT SO THE COACH LET ME COME HOME FOR A FEW MINUTES!

YOU'D BETTER PLAN TO BE THERE, TOO, DAD. A LOT OF MAJOR LEAGUE SCOUTS ARE SUPPOSED TO BE THERE, AND MY COACH SAYS SEVERAL WANT TO DRAFT ME. SINCE YOU'RE GOING TO BE MY BUSINESS MANAGER, THEY MIGHT WANT TO SEE YOU!

I'LL BE THERE... AND DROP A FEW HINTS THAT WE'LL EXPECT A BONUS FOR SIGNING!

YIPPEE! A MAJOR LEAGUER! MY BROTHER'S GOING TO BE A BIG LEAGUER!

HOLD IT, TIMMY, FIRST OF ALL I HAVE TO GET THAT CONTRACT...THEN THERE'LL BE SOME TIME IN THE MINORS. BUT I'LL MAKE IT ALL THE WAY---I KNOW I WILL!

OF COURSE YOU WILL, SON... BUT HOW ABOUT SOME DINNER? HAVE YOU --

NO, THANKS, MOM. WE HAD A SNACK RIGHT AFTER THE TEAM PULLED INTO TOWN. I'M TOO EXCITED ANYWAY!

THEN WHY DON'T ALL OF YOU GO TO THE FAMILY ROOM, AND I'LL GET SOME DESSERT READY!

YES, GARY...WE'VE BEEN TALKING ABOUT DRUGS. I'LL BET YOU KNOW A LOT ABOUT THEM. KIDS USE THEM IN COLLEGE, DON'T THEY?

SOME DO, BUT AT OUR COLLEGE THEY'RE BEGINING TO WISE UP TO HOW STUPID IT IS TO FOOL AROUND WITH DRUGS. FOR SOME OF THEM THOUGH, IT'S TOO LATE. THEY'RE HOOKED!

JUST WHAT'S IT LIKE TO BE HOOKED? IS IT HARD TO STOP TAKING DRUGS?

THAT'S RIGHT, SUSAN. A KID WHO'S HOOKED IS A LOT LIKE AN ALCOHOLIC WHO CAN'T DO WITHOUT LIQUOR. THEY BOTH WIND UP SICK -- SICK AND HARD TO HELP!

WELL, I'VE GOT A PROBLEM, GARY. HOW AM I GOING TO SAY "NO" WHEN THE GUYS ASK ME TO SMOKE MARIJUANA OR TAKE PEP PILLS OR SOMETHING? WHAT IF THEY CALL ME "CHICKEN"?

LET THEM, TIMMY!

I'LL TELL YOU WHAT HAPPENED TO ME A COUPLE OF YEARS AGO. I MET REEP AND TONY ONE NIGHT -- BOTH HIGH ON MARIJUANA -- AND THEY WANTED ME TO SMOKE IT. BUT I SAID NO. DRUGS AND CAREERS DON'T MIX.

"...BELIEVE ME, IT WASN'T EASY TO TAKE A LOT OF GUFF FROM A COUPLE OF CREEPS LIKE THAT, BUT I DID..."

YOU'RE JUST A BIG SHOWOFF, GARY. NO GUTS! YOU'RE A MAKE-BELIEVE ATHLETE!

YEAH, GARY... YOU'RE CHICKEN, CHICKEN!

AND YOU LET THEM GET AWAY WITH THAT TALK? WHY, GARY, YOU COULD LICK BOTH OF THOSE BUMS AT ONCE!

YES, TIMMY,.. AND WITH ONE HAND TIED BEHIND MY BACK! BUT REMEMBER THIS; WHEN IT COMES TO DRUGS, IT'S THE ONE WHO IS CHICKEN WHO CALLS ANOTHER A NAME LIKE THAT! GUYS LIKE REEP AND TONY USE DRUGS AS A CRUTCH TO LEAN ON BECAUSE THEY'RE WEAK AND AFRAID OF LIFE!

GARY, ARE YOU TALKING ABOUT "REEP THE CREEP"? I KNOW HIM. HE'S GROSS!

YES, THAT'S WHAT THEY CALL HIM NOW... "REEP THE CREEP". I SAW HIM THE LAST TIME I WAS HOME FROM COLLEGE. HE'S HOOKED NOW, POOR FELLOW, AND WHAT A SAD CASE...

"... YES, HE'S THE SAME GUY WHO THOUGHT HE WAS BEING SMART USING DRUGS AND TRYING TO RUN DOWN OTHER PEOPLE WHO DIDN'T..."

"... BUT UNLESS POOR REEP CAN SOMEHOW PULL HIMSELF TOGETHER, THERE'S NOT MUCH LEFT IN LIFE FOR HIM TO LOOK FORWARD TO -- NOTHING BUT MISERY AND TOMORROW'S JOB OF GETTING MORE DRUGS TO FEED HIS ADDICTION!"

CAN'T ANYTHING BE DONE TO HELP PEOPLE DEPENDENT ON DRUGS TO GET OFF THEM?

I'LL ANSWER THAT ONE, SUSAN. IT DEPENDS ON THE INDIVIDUAL. PHYSICAL DEPENDENCE ON ALL DRUGS CAN BE OVERCOME. THE TOUGHEST PART OF DRUG DEPENDENCE IS RIGHT IN A PERSON'S OWN MIND!

IT'S THE UNSURE PERSON -- ONE WHO IS AFRAID TO FACE LIFE -- WHO TURNS TO DRUGS IN THE FIRST PLACE. IT TAKES A PERSON OF STRONG WILL TO STRAIGHTEN UP AND KICK THE HABIT, BUT SOME ARE ABLE TO DO IT!

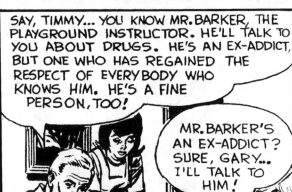

SAY, TIMMY... YOU KNOW MR. BARKER, THE PLAYGROUND INSTRUCTOR. HE'LL TALK TO YOU ABOUT DRUGS. HE'S AN EX-ADDICT, BUT ONE WHO HAS REGAINED THE RESPECT OF EVERYBODY WHO KNOWS HIM. HE'S A FINE PERSON, TOO!

MR. BARKER'S AN EX-ADDICT? SURE, GARY... I'LL TALK TO HIM!

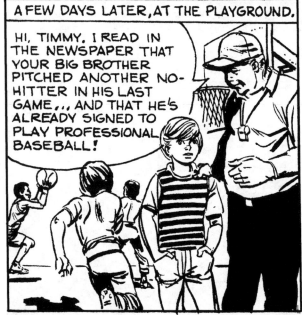

A FEW DAYS LATER, AT THE PLAYGROUND.

HI, TIMMY. I READ IN THE NEWSPAPER THAT YOUR BIG BROTHER PITCHED ANOTHER NO-HITTER IN HIS LAST GAME... AND THAT HE'S ALREADY SIGNED TO PLAY PROFESSIONAL BASEBALL!

YOU CAN BE MIGHTY PROUD OF HIM, TIMMY, HE'S A FINE YOUNG MAN!

HE THINKS YOU'RE PRETTY SWELL, TOO MR. BARKER. HE WAS HOME THE NIGHT BEFORE THE GAME. WE WERE TALKING ABOUT DRUGS AND HE SAID...

WELL, ER, HE SAID --

HE SAID I'M AN EX-ADDICT, DIDN'T HE? WELL, IT'S TRUE, AND I WANT TO HELP OTHERS. I JUST HOPE I CAN KEEP A LOT OF NICE KIDS FROM GOING WRONG THE WAY I DID!

MR. BARKER, COULD I CALL HANK AND STEVE OVER HERE TO TALK WITH US? I WANT THEM TO HEAR WHAT YOU HAVE TO SAY!

OF COURSE, TIMMY, CALL THEM!

MR. BARKER TELLS THE BOYS ABOUT THE DIFFERENT KINDS OF DRUGS -- PEP PILLS (AMPHETAMINES), TRANQUILIZERS AND SLEEPING PILLS (MOST OF WHICH ARE BARBITURATES) AND HARD NARCOTICS, SUCH AS HEROIN...

HOW ABOUT GLUE SNIFFING? IT WON'T HURT YOU, WILL IT?

ANY DRUG -- ANY CHEMICAL -- THAT IS MISUSED CAN BE DANGEROUS! GLUE, PEP PILLS, SLEEPING PILLS -- ANY OF THEM, WHEN MISUSED, CAN BE BAD!

AND NEARLY ALL OF THE YOUNG PEOPLE WHO ARE ON THE HARD STUFF BEGAN BY EXPERIMENTING WITH DRUGS LIKE THESE AND WITH MARIJUANA.

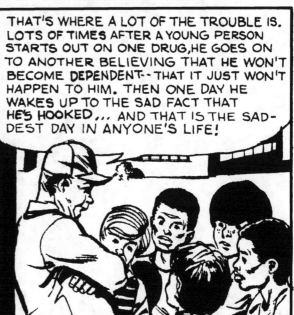

THAT'S WHERE A LOT OF THE TROUBLE IS. LOTS OF TIMES AFTER A YOUNG PERSON STARTS OUT ON ONE DRUG, HE GOES ON TO ANOTHER BELIEVING THAT HE WON'T BECOME DEPENDENT -- THAT IT JUST WON'T HAPPEN TO HIM. THEN ONE DAY HE WAKES UP TO THE SAD FACT THAT HE'S HOOKED,... AND THAT IS THE SADDEST DAY IN ANYONE'S LIFE!

IF YOU LOOKED THE WHOLE WORLD OVER, YOU'D PROBABLY NEVER FIND AN ADDICT, IF HE'S HONEST, WHO ISN'T SORRY THAT HE EVER GOT MIXED UP WITH DRUGS!

GEE, MR. BARKER, I'M GLAD YOU'VE TOLD US ABOUT DRUGS 'CAUSE YOU REALLY KNOW WHAT THEY'RE LIKE. BUT WHAT IF A GUY HAS ALREADY STARTED... A LITTLE, MAYBE?

THEN STOP, HANK, STOP BEFORE IT'S TOO LATE!

THE TROUBLE IS THAT THOSE WHO HAVE STARTED ON DRUGS FIGURE THAT JUST ONCE MORE WON'T HURT, BUT AFTER THAT, THERE'S ANOTHER TIME, THEN ANOTHER. THERE'S REALLY ONLY ONE SENSIBLE ANSWER---

I KNOW WHAT THAT IS, MR. BARKER...

I'M GOING TO BE LIKE MY BIG BROTHER, GARY. HE SAYS AS LONG AS YOU'VE NEVER MISUSED DRUGS THE FIRST TIME... NOT EVEN ONCE... THEN THERE'S NOTHING TO WORRY ABOUT. I'LL NEVER USE THEM!

NEVER?

NO, HANK, **NEVER!** NOT EVEN IF THEY CALL ME "CHICKEN"!

PURE IMAGINATION ON THE WEB

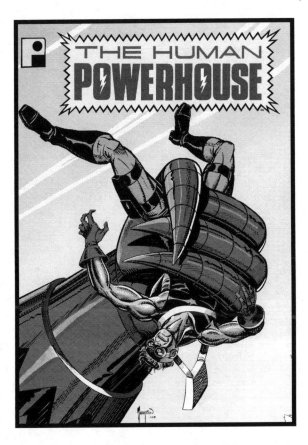

MEET GREG THEAKSTON'S
HUMAN
POWERHOUSE
Free Online
·
The P.I. Bookstore
·
Free Comics Downloads
·
The Theakston Gallery
·
http://pureimagination.info

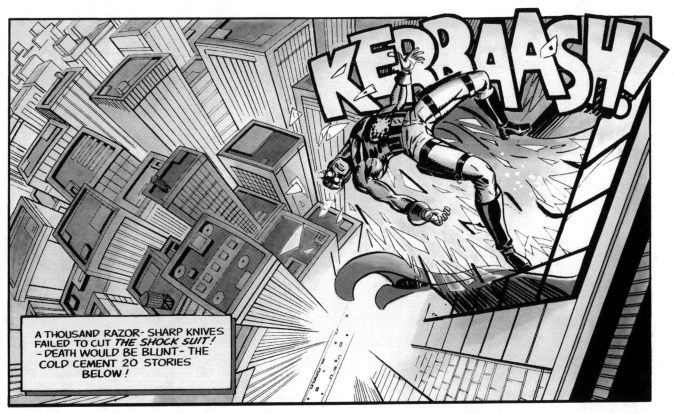

A THOUSAND RAZOR-SHARP KNIVES FAILED TO CUT *THE SHOCK SUIT!* - DEATH WOULD BE BLUNT - THE COLD CEMENT 20 STORIES BELOW!